Church Growth in Mexico

Church Growth in Mexico

1368

by
DONALD McGAVRAN
Director, The Institute of Church Growth

JOHN HUEGEL
Missionary in Mexico

JACK TAYLOR
Graduate Fellow, The Institute of Church Growth

WM. B. EERDMANS PUBLISHING COMPANY
GRAND RAPIDS, MICHIGAN

Foreword

Today Latin America is constantly being called to our attention. We recognize the fact that we of the United States have not been fully aware of the economic, political, and cultural importance of the countries of Latin America to the United States and the world. Nor have we been fully aware that the political and economic policies of the United States have oftentimes been misunderstood and unacceptable to Latin America. The Latin American peoples are being rediscovered; hurried attempts are being made to help the peoples and governments to political stability, economic security, and social justice. We are learning that economic, political, and social independence and dignity are worthy and just goals of the Latin American peoples.

A vast wealth of information is now being presented to the interested North American through books, magazine articles, radio and TV presentations. The religious situation in Latin America, however, is still largely unknown by the North American reader. Perhaps the most interesting phenomenon in the religious world of today is the development of the Protestant movement in Latin America during the last thirty years. It is estimated that at the present time, 7,000,000, or 3½ percent of the 200,000,000 population, in Latin America are Protestants, better known as *"Evangélicos"* in Latin America. Little consideration in the past has been given to the reasons for this phenomenal development, or perhaps of greater importance, the reasons for a rapid growth in some places and no growth in others.

Church Growth in Mexico is such a study of the development of the Protestant Churches in Mexico. One of its values is that the study is limited to one country, Mexico. It is often forgotten that conditions vary greatly from one country to another and that it is difficult to make any general statement that is equally true for all of Latin America. Even so, *Church Growth in Mexico* presents principles and suggests policies that are applicable in other areas.

Mexico has the largest population of the Spanish-speaking countries in Latin America, with approximately 35,000,000 inhabitants. While Mexico is a part of North America geographically, it is Latin American culturally and historically. Anyone that visits Mexico, and especially the capital city, is tremendously impressed with the rich culture of the Mexican people. Mexico is one of the few countries in Latin America that has undergone its social revolution. The steady development in the economic, educational, and social aspects of the Mexican revolution presents a stability in the political and economic life of Mexico that bespeaks the large role that Mexico is to play in the future of the American nations. The authors of this book wisely chose Mexico for the study of the development of the Protestant movement.

For the study, the authors have made an interesting division of the country into ten different Mexicos, not geographically, but based on the different principles related to church growth. An analysis is made of the factors that tend to cause static churches, and those that definitely produce a growing church. Any worker in a Latin American country, or even in the United States, can recognize characteristics of his own congregation or churches with which he may be related, as he reads Chapters 5 and 6. The "case studies" are not only statements of historical development, but also exemplify principles that a reader can apply to the church with which he may be related.

The reader may find that he does not agree with the theology of the study, or the emphasis on evangelism, or the inferences about social and educational work. This should not, however, permit him to miss the fundamental message of the book. For regardless of how effective a church may be in its educational, social, or community program, if it is not definitely increasing its outreach with the message of Christ to new people who accept Him as Lord, then the church is already a static institution, or in grave danger of becoming so. The Church of Christ is basically a missionary Church.

I enjoyed reading the book and trust it will find a wide acceptance by our church leaders. It deserves careful reading and consideration.

HOWARD W. YODER, *Executive Secretary*
Committee on Cooperation in Latin America
National Council of the Churches of Christ

New York, New York

Introduction

This book intends to illuminate the church-growth problem: what makes churches grow and stop growing among the thirty-three million inhabitants of Mexico. It compares church growth which has been granted to and achieved by the various denominations, examines church and mission history and the activities of Mexican churchmen and missionaries as these bear upon the multiplication of churches, and reaches behind clichés of modern mission — the superficial, commonly alleged reasons for church growth — to the basic ones.

This report assumes that Christian mission in Mexico is an urgent necessity, a command of the Lord Jesus, and it intends to inform those who already believe this of the real progress in discipling the peoples of Mexico. A good way to forward Christ's purposes in Mexico is to give a picture of the true state of the enterprise.

Church Growth in Mexico reflects the "church growth" point of view. The three men whose joint labors produced this book share a dynamic view of the growth of the Church. Each takes church growth seriously, considering it a chief and irreplaceable part of the task of the Church.

Rev. John Huegel is a second-generation missionary in Mexico who knows the Evangelical Church, speaks Spanish fluently, has become a citizen of Mexico, and has friends among leaders of many denominations. He contributed Chapter 7 and had a large part in the rest of the book through sharing his insights and information during a field trip in Mexico in the summer of 1962 and critically reviewing and correcting the manuscript in the fall of that year. Rev. Jack Taylor, a graduate fellow of the Institute of Church Growth, assembled much of the information in

Chapter 2. He made a careful study of the *braceros,* now published under the title *God's Messengers to Mexico's Masses* and available from the Institute of Church Growth. All our references to the *braceros* and their influence on church growth depend on Mr. Taylor's findings.

The remaining chapters come from my hand. In a real sense what I have written comes not from me but from a multitude of churchmen in Mexico (nationals and missionaries) who have been frank in discussing the growth of their congregations and denominations. My function has been chiefly that of assembling in one ordered whole what many are thinking about church growth and have been kind enough to share with me. I owe them a debt of gratitude for taking time to describe to the Huegel-Taylor-McGavran party the quality and quantity of church growth they have been granted.

In order to study church growth, it is necessary to ask basic questions. What is the Evangelical Church (Church of Christ) in Mexico? What are its Branches? Which are growing and why? Which are static and why? What mission policies encourage church growth? Which prevent it? Which theological and ecclesiastical traditions and customs of North American Protestant churches favor church growth in Mexico and which are detrimental to it? What bearing has the agrarian revolt on the growth of the Evangelical faith? This book has been written to cast light on these questions. It may be regarded as a pioneer effort to see the problem as a whole across denominational lines and to apply to church growth in Mexico some of the insights being gained in other lands.

A clear understanding of the complex processes by which it has pleased God to increase His churches is obviously necessary. Getting that understanding is an enterprise of high import. If this study stimulates more serious, factual, and detailed assessments of the factors which in Mexico promote or impede church growth, its purpose will have been achieved.

We invite others to stand on our shoulders and see further than we have been able to do.

August 1, 1963

DONALD MCGAVRAN

The Institute of Church Growth
Eugene, Oregon, U.S.A.

Contents

13

1 The Puzzle Presented by Mexico — and Theology

The following graph presents the puzzle of the Evangelical Church in Mexico. The contrast between the great growth achieved by some sections of the Church and the limited growth of others is clearly apparent.

The lowest line on the graph represents the membership in Mexico of the Christian Church (Disciples of Christ), a large, aggressive North American Church with a highly organized foreign missions program. Though assisted most of the time by a dozen missionaries and considerable funds, the total membership has grown, declined, and grown again, from 485 in 1915 to 972 in 1960.

The next line represents the Southern Baptists, a vital, powerful Church in the United States with a vigorous foreign missions program. Mexico has been one of its major fields for over fifty years. Yet its Church, too, showed little growth until 1950. For forty years it plateaued at about 3000. Since 1950 it has grown steadily. See the upturn in the graph.

The top line shows a very different type of growth. It soars to 278,000 full members. Since these are accompanied by unbaptized believers and sympathizers, numbering possibly another 200,000, and the children of all three classifications, an Evangelical Community of possibly a million has been created in the last fifty years. Some Branches of the Church have been getting good growth. Some have not.

Are these lines of growth reliable?

Membership figures in Mexico, as well as in other lands, vary considerably. Figures for any one year might be in error for any one of a number of different reasons; but with annual figures, the general trend of growth is highly reliable.

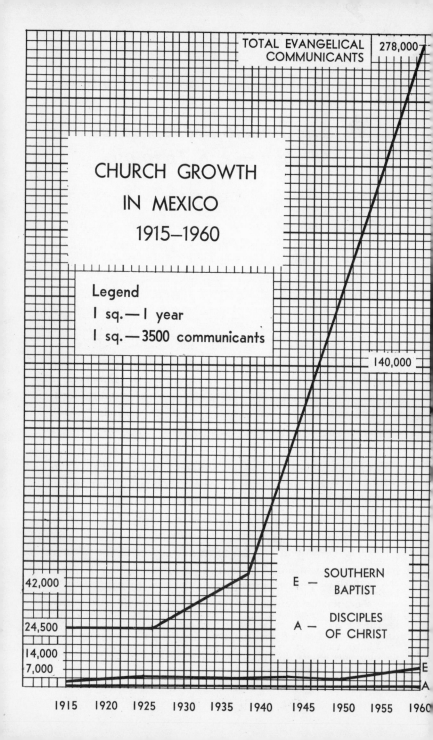

Errors of one year will be rectified the next. The general growth picture portrayed by these three lines is indisputable.

In the next chapter we shall see the membership figures for many different denominations in the various states of the Republic of Mexico. These figures will bear out this first impression and show that many missions have been relatively static in a land where the Church of Christ[1] as a whole has grown well.

The puzzle cannot be solved easily by invoking the myth of a "difficult land" — though the popularity of the myth is natural enough and some sections of Mexico are resistant to the missionary work of the Church. Some denominations, with great sacrifices and toil, established little bands of Evangelicals in cities, towns and villages; but these remained static worshiping groups of 20, 30, 40, or (at mission stations) of 80 to 200. In some villages lone families maintained the Evangelical spark for years. Inevitably, missionaries and Mexican ministers associated with these efforts have thought theirs "an Islamic land" where, because of the fanaticism of the population, their church really could not grow. Generations of missionaries, in mission after mission, have served in Mexico and seen only a few baptisms. Their church — they thought — did well to survive. It did "a good work." It "witnessed for Christ." It bore persecution bravely. It "served the people" through education, agriculture, and medicine. But it did not proliferate. The spark was there, but it lit no fire.

True as all this is, in the same nation other denomina-

---

1 In this book we speak of "the Church of Christ" as synonymous with "the Protestant Church" or "the Evangelical Church." We use Evangelical Churches, Protestant Churches, Church of Christ and its Branches, and Evangelical Faith as meaning the same thing. Disciples of Christ might be expected to stress the underlying unity of the Church. At the same time, since in practice Americans commonly speak of individual Churches (the Presbyterian Church or the Baptist Church), we do not hesitate on occasion to speak of the Methodist Church, the Mennonite Church, or the Otomi Church. When capitalized, Church means either the Church Universal or a denomination. When not capitalized, church means congregation, or it is used as an adjective, i.e., church government.

tions grew greatly.   Mexico did not prove to be an Islamic
land to them.   Their sparks did light fires.

A further aspect of the puzzle is that, while Mexico has
carried out a successful social revolution in a land where the
Church of Rome and the landed classes were united in ex-
ploiting the masses and keeping them ignorant, landless, and
in subjection, this social revolution has not led to a Reformation of the Roman Catholic Church.   No large exodus has
occurred.   The common people of Mexico have been rather
successful in breaking their political chains, but the Church
of Christ has nowhere successfully linked social revolution
with the Evangelical Faith.   Although Protestants are commonly considered as connected in some way with progress,
and although political liberals have been favorable to the
Evangelical cause, and agrarian revolutionists have occasionally espoused the Evangelical Faith, the multitudes demanding
social justice have not recognized the Evangelical Faith as
their fundamental rationale — as their religious base.

Some leaders in the Roman Catholic Church have loudly
proclaimed that Protestants and Communists are one and the
same people, though the clergy knows this to be untrue.   But
despite the patent fact that the only countries in the world
where Marxist communism has no hold are the Protestant
countries, the Evangelical Churches have not been able to
affirm an undying hostility to the mechanical atheistic communism of Russia together with an equally undying certainty
that the spread of the Church of Christ gives a just society
its only true foundation.   This is part of the puzzle of Mexico.

Some readers might like to turn from the puzzle of church
growth in Mexico by denying its significance.   They feel
superior to quantitative considerations and say they are not
interested in "mere numbers."

Their feeling may rise (1) *from the close confinement of
Christian mission to unresponsive populations.*   Perhaps they
have worked for many years in a field where few became
Christians and have, in consequence, decided that witness
for Christ is the essential thing and that it really makes little

difference how many become His disciples. Only by some such reasoning could they have remained patiently preaching Christ to a resistant population. They universalize their experience into a rule for all mission.

Or this feeling may arise (2) *from a humanitarian view of mission.* If they believe Christian mission consists in helping people grow more corn, keep better cattle, achieve a higher standard of living, and become better educated citizens of this one world, then the number of confessed Christians is, for them, of scant significance.

Or it may arise (3) *from theological considerations.* Some Christians believe that since Christ is concerned with the salvation of individuals, each of infinite value, the number of Christians and churches is not important. "How can you measure the transformation of a man's life!" they exclaim.

What does theology say to these responses to membership statistics?

Theology would begin, I think, with the third point and agree that Christ yearns for the salvation of individuals. He died that men and women might have eternal life. The infinite value of each person rests, ultimately, on the fact that Jesus Christ died for him. He went to the cross for all men — Africans, Asians, and Latin Americans, as well as Europeans and Americans. This fact makes it all the more imperative to take growth statistics seriously. The cross itself will not allow us to say that the number of persons won to Christ is of no importance. There is no such thing as "mere numbers." Each number represents a person of infinite value. The more persons won, the better pleased is God. This is bedrock in Christian mission. The entire New Testament and the Church bear witness to it.

To the second point (the humanitarian understanding of mission), Christian theology would say this: because of what Jesus our Lord did to help men, mission may legitimately try to help people, but helping people is no substitute for reconciling them to God. Christian theology would press home the point that Jesus Christ in His earthly life healed, fed, and helped men; but, instead of prolonging His earthly life so that He could continue to feed multitudes, He terminated it after a brief service so that salvation might be made available to all who believed. Luke records (5:16) that when multitudes gathered to be healed, "he withdrew" and went to a lonely place to pray. The Christian, like his Master, has priorities.

Christian theology would insist that Christian mission is the duty and privilege of all Christians, regardless of their economic status. A church of poor people might carry on mission to rich people. Christian mission is what the "have nots" can carry to all people — to educated, powerful and cultured unbelievers, and to illiterate, weak and uncultured unbelievers. Christian mission does not preach the gospel of a full dinner pail, or a better economic system; though Christian mission does feed the hungry.

To those who (so that they may stay on and labor in "difficult fields") are not interested in the number of Christians won, Christian theology would reply: We believe that the gospel must be preached to all men, resistant as well as responsive, and that the number of the redeemed is important. Some shepherds, who search all day for the lost and return home with nothing to show for their labor, will, indeed, merit a "well done" from the Good Shepherd; but this truth must not be twisted into an assertion that the Good Shepherd sends men out to conduct a fruitless search and really cares nothing about how many are found. We dare not, on theological grounds, affirm that coming empty handed out of ripe harvest fields, pleases God, or that He desires "grateful witness from the redeemed" more than He does the objective finding of the lost. The Lord of the Harvest counts the sheaves. The Good Shepherd rejoices in multitudes found.

In short, we present the next two chapters — columns and tables — believing they have theological significance. The assertion sometimes encountered that a small Church is necessarily better, since it is interested in quality not quantity, is not only a rationalization of defeat, it is theologically untenable. A non-growing Church which does not reach out to bring to the Saviour the teeming multitudes which surround it lacks vital Christian quality. A Church which is always pressing on among its fellows to reconcile them to God in Christ has both quantity and quality. Indeed, quantity and quality are not antithetical terms. They supplement each other. True quality, in a responsive population, will lead to church growth. And church growth bears eloquent witness that the Christians concerned share the heart of the Saviour.

Since theology is interested in numbers and in growth, the puzzle becomes even more puzzling. How does it happen, we ask, that ardent Christians — nationals and missionaries — at work in Mexico have seen their labors accompanied by such spotty growth? Why then do such variations in church growth occur? The columns, we believe, have significance to God and to His Church.

2 A Columnar Picture by States

by Jack Taylor and Donald McGavran

Light is cast on the Church of Christ in Mexico when we regard it denominationally and geographically. The following groups of columns indicate at a glance the relative size of the Branches of the Church in 29 main sections of Mexico — 28 states and 1 territory. The names of the states appear from left to right across the bottom of each graph. Each state has rising from it a cluster of columns representing the membership of the denominations found there. The names of the denominations are at the top of the sheet.

The map shows where the states are, so that the border states, the southern states, and others can be readily located.

This columnar picture is intended to give a vivid impression of the spottiness of church growth in Mexico. Look at San Luis Potosi. Seven denominations are "at work" there. Three have tiny memberships of less than 200. Two have 300 - 350. One has a little over 800 and one soars to 5200. Look at Vera Cruz. The Church of God (Tennessee) and the Seventh-day Adventists have about 2200 and about 5000 respectively, but the rest who reported have very small memberships.

This columnar picture gives a true impression. It is not, however, a census and must not be used in that way. The figures are taken from Dr. Clyde Taylor's recent book.[1] Taylor and Coggins were dependent on figures sent to them. Since it is difficult to get membership figures from some Branches

1 C. E. Taylor and W. T. Coggins, *Protestant Missions in Latin America,* (Evangelical Foreign Missions Association, 1962).

of the Church, the columnar picture is far from complete. For example, the Independent Presbyterian Mexican Church, the Apostolic Church, and others are not portrayed because they did not supply membership figures by states. Furthermore, since denominations do not ordinarily break down their all-Mexico figures into state figures, these latter, when estimated, are now and then inaccurate. For example, the Presbyterians in Tabasco are listed as 3600, though my own investigations (see Chapter 8) make me think 7000 to 12,000 a more realistic figure. Then, too, when a membership is found in two states, few denominational secretaries know exactly how many of the members of their churches are in each state, though their all-Mexico total will be quite accurate.

Furthermore, churchmen in Mexico are quick to point out that membership figures are often approximations. Definitions of membership change. One minister will count Christmas and Easter Christians as full members. The next will count only those who attend regularly and contribute to the church. Some churches have a category called "unbaptized believers." Others call this same category "unbaptized members."

Any one column may be in error for any one of these or other reasons. And there are certainly omissions. Yet the general impression given by these columns is correct. Subject to the qualifications of the succeeding paragraphs, this columnar picture is what the Branches of the Church of Christ in Mexico in each state look like. We trust no one will look for omissions and inaccuracies so diligently that he will miss the main picture.

Note that in the states of the northern border — Tamaulipas, Nuevo Leon, Coahuila, Chihuahua, and Sonora — where the population is larger and much movement to and from the United States takes place, some columns are tall, i.e., church growth has been greater than in Mexico's heart, the high, cool Meseta Central.

1   FEDERAL DISTRICT
2   MORELOS
3   TLAXCALA
4   COLIMA
5   PUEBLA
6   AGUASCALIENTES
7   MEXICO
8   HIDALGO
9   QUERETARO
10 GUANAJUATO
11 NAYARIT

THE STATES OF MEXICO

NUEVO LEON

TAMAULIPAS

POTOSI

9

8

7

1

2

3

5

VERA
CRUZ

GUERRERO

OAXACA

CHIAPAS

TABASCO

CAMPECHE

QUINTANA ROO

YUCATAN

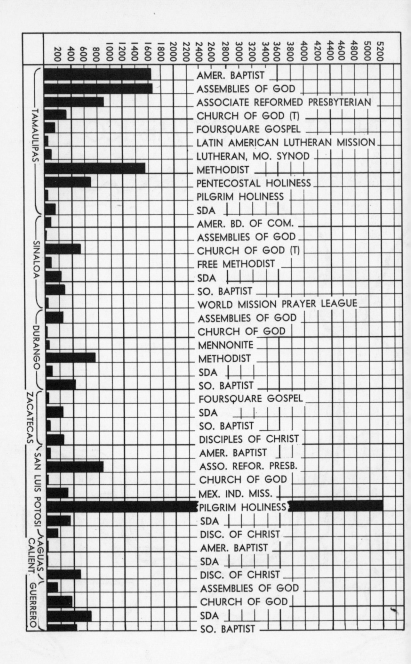

Scale (top): 200 400 600 800 1000 1200 1400 1600 1800 2000 2200 2400 2600 2800 3000 3200 3400 3600 3800 4000 4200 4400 4600 4800 5000 5200

TAMAULIPAS
- AMER. BAPTIST
- ASSEMBLIES OF GOD
- ASSOCIATE REFORMED PRESBYTERIAN
- CHURCH OF GOD (T)
- FOURSQUARE GOSPEL
- LATIN AMERICAN LUTHERAN MISSION
- LUTHERAN, MO. SYNOD
- METHODIST
- PENTECOSTAL HOLINESS
- PILGRIM HOLINESS
- SDA

SINALOA
- AMER. BD. OF COM.
- ASSEMBLIES OF GOD
- CHURCH OF GOD (T)
- FREE METHODIST
- SDA
- SO. BAPTIST
- WORLD MISSION PRAYER LEAGUE

DURANGO
- ASSEMBLIES OF GOD
- CHURCH OF GOD
- MENNONITE
- METHODIST
- SDA
- SO. BAPTIST

ZACATECAS
- FOURSQUARE GOSPEL
- SDA
- SO. BAPTIST

SAN LUIS POTOSI
- DISCIPLES OF CHRIST
- AMER. BAPTIST
- ASSO. REFOR. PRESB.
- CHURCH OF GOD
- MEX. IND. MISS.
- PILGRIM HOLINESS
- SDA
- DISC. OF CHRIST

AGUAS CALIENT.
- AMER. BAPTIST
- SDA
- DISC. OF CHRIST

GUERRERO
- ASSEMBLIES OF GOD
- CHURCH OF GOD
- SDA
- SO. BAPTIST

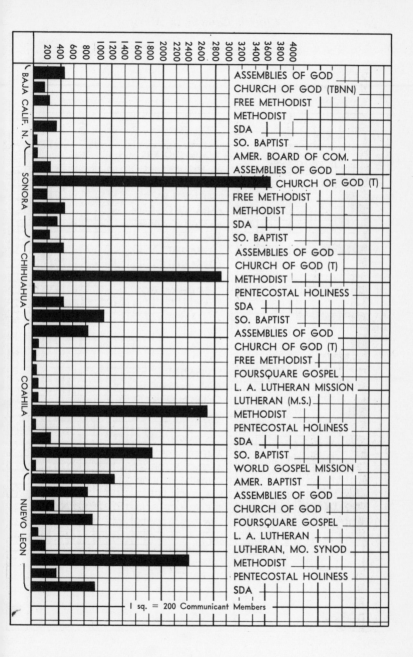

The chart displays the following scale across the top: 200, 400, 600, 800, 1000, 1200, 1400, 1600, 1800, 2000, 2200, 2400, 2600, 2800, 3000, 3200, 3400, 3600, 3800, 4000

BAJA CALIF. N.
- ASSEMBLIES OF GOD
- CHURCH OF GOD (TBNN)
- FREE METHODIST
- METHODIST
- SDA
- SO. BAPTIST
- AMER. BOARD OF COM.

SONORA
- ASSEMBLIES OF GOD
- CHURCH OF GOD (T)
- FREE METHODIST
- METHODIST
- SDA
- SO. BAPTIST

CHIHUAHUA
- ASSEMBLIES OF GOD
- CHURCH OF GOD (T)
- METHODIST
- PENTECOSTAL HOLINESS
- SDA
- SO. BAPTIST

COAHILA
- ASSEMBLIES OF GOD
- CHURCH OF GOD (T)
- FREE METHODIST
- FOURSQUARE GOSPEL
- L. A. LUTHERAN MISSION
- LUTHERAN (M.S.)
- METHODIST
- PENTECOSTAL HOLINESS
- SDA
- SO. BAPTIST

NUEVO LEON
- WORLD GOSPEL MISSION
- AMER. BAPTIST
- ASSEMBLIES OF GOD
- CHURCH OF GOD
- FOURSQUARE GOSPEL
- L. A. LUTHERAN
- LUTHERAN, MO. SYNOD
- METHODIST
- PENTECOSTAL HOLINESS
- SDA

1 sq. = 200 Communicant Members

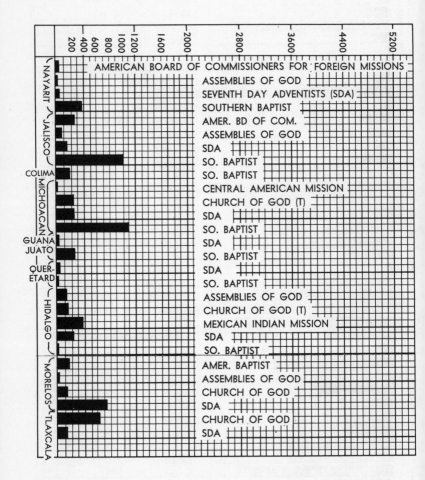

AMERICAN BOARD OF COMMISSIONERS FOR FOREIGN MISSIONS
ASSEMBLIES OF GOD
SEVENTH DAY ADVENTISTS (SDA)
SOUTHERN BAPTIST
AMER. BD OF COM.
ASSEMBLIES OF GOD
SDA
SO. BAPTIST
SO. BAPTIST
CENTRAL AMERICAN MISSION
CHURCH OF GOD (T)
SDA
SO. BAPTIST
SDA
SO. BAPTIST
SDA
SO. BAPTIST
ASSEMBLIES OF GOD
CHURCH OF GOD (T)
MEXICAN INDIAN MISSION
SDA
SO. BAPTIST
AMER. BAPTIST
ASSEMBLIES OF GOD
CHURCH OF GOD
SDA
CHURCH OF GOD
SDA

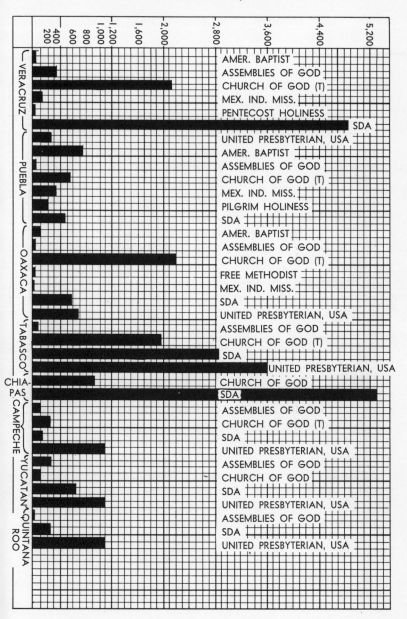

In the southern states also the Church of Christ has grown well.

In the Federal District, including Mexico City, the Church is commonly said to have grown best of all. In this great city of five million souls, one in forty is believed to be an Evangelical. According to this estimate, Mexico City would have an Evangelical population of 125,000, or more than half the Evangelicals of the entire country. Because some of the numerous columns here would be so tall as to run off the graph, the Federal District including Mexico City has been omitted from this pictorial presentation.

Note the states with a tiny Evangelical population — Baja California North, Zacatecas, and Jalisco, for example.

Observe the large number of missions whose Church consists of a few score Christians: Two Lutheran missions, for example, in Tamaulipas, each having less than 100 members, although others in that state have 1400 communicants and more. Mexico has many small missions which are not planting much church!

Here and there in a general paucity of growth one column will shoot up to two, three, or four thousand (see the columns for Oaxaca, San Luis Potosi, and Sonora). This means that some denomination has met a responsive homogeneous unit in a generally irresponsive population. A small people movement has taken place, or a vigorous Christian surge has swept across one part of the population.

Though this columnar picture is helpful to our understanding, it should be revised by some future writer. Accurate figures from several large denominations now missing should be entered. When state totals and national totals for all the Pentecostal denominations are known, the columnar picture will better represent the Evangelical Church in Mexico. The revision will show, we believe, more and larger columns along the border, in the Federal District including Mexico City, and in some other responsive areas, as well as a scattering of more small columns throughout the land — even in the more resistant and fanatical states. It will em-

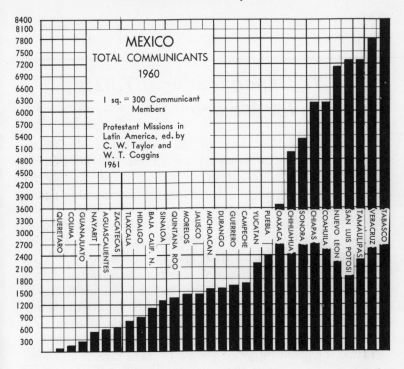

MEXICO
TOTAL COMMUNICANTS
1960

1 sq. = 300 Communicant
Members

Protestant Missions in
Latin America, ed. by
C. W. Taylor and
W. T. Coggins
1961

phasize the spotty nature of church growth and increase the
contrast between the growing and the non-growing Branches
of the Church of Christ.

Of special note is the last columnar graph, called "Mexico, Total Communicants 1960." It illustrates vividly the
states in which responsiveness plus serious church planting
have together produced substantial church growth and the
states where indifference or hostility, plus many kinds of
splendid mission activity, have together produced a few hundred Evangelicals in all the Branches of the Church of Christ
put together.

The columnar representation of this chapter, then, does
not solve the puzzle of church growth in Mexico. Rather, it
makes even more apparent the real nature of the situation
and leaves us with an even greater *why* than did Chapter 1.

3 Denominational Totals for Mexico

Each denomination exists in the geographical distribution portrayed by the columnar representations. Having seen the "state-wise shape" of the denominations in Mexico, we are now ready to observe the denominational membership figures *for the country as a whole.*

The following figures were supplied by Rev. Gustavo Velasco, head of Casa Unida de Publicaciones, at 24 C Chile, Mexico D. F., in August 1962. He and the National Council of Evangelical Churches of Mexico have been working on a census, and he has presented us with the following figures as the most reliable available today. For the most part, he obtained official figures from appropriate authorities in each denomination. In a few cases where he could not get firm figures, he asked informed people to make careful estimates.

TABLE I

SIGNIFICANT MEXICO-WIDE SUMMARIES

CHURCHES	Churches with buildings	2,802	
	Churches without buildings	813	
	Churches duly organized		3,615
	Missions (churchlets) w/bldg.	939	
	Missions without buildings	1,801	
	Total missions		2,740
	Grand total churches and missions		6,355
STAFF	Ministers ordained	2,135	
	Ministers unordained	1,616	
	Deaconesses	204	
	Other workers	2,071	
	National missionaries	47	
	Foreign missionaries	515	
	Preseminary ministerial students	120	
	Seminarians	481	

Students for other Christian serv.   104
                        Grand total staff   7,293

MEMBERSHIP   60% Pentecostal
            Total full members   249,851   (150,000 Pen-
                                                             tecostal
                                                             100,000 other
                                                             Evangelicals)

            Total children members   107,121
            Grand total Protestants   356,972

TABLE II

COMMUNICANTS BY DENOMINATIONS

PENTECOSTALS		OTHERS	V*	T*
Interdenominational	27,000	Presbyterian	37,000	66,000
Independent Evangelical	20,000	Ind. Presby. Mexican	1,000	
Swedish Pentecostals	15,000	Ind. Presby. USA	5,000	
Assemblies of God	10,000	Methodist	28,000	11,000
Miepi	10,000	Ind. Methodists	5,000	
Assemblies of God II	5,000	Southern Baptists	9,000	9,000
Apostolics	9,000	American Baptists	5,000	6,000
Church of God (Foursquare)	10,000	Ind. Baptists	3,000	
Others	40,000	Reformed Ass. Presby.	3,000	
Total	146,000	Christian Churches	1,000	
Pentecostal total	146,000	Lutherans (Mexican)	1,000	
Others total	129,700	Missouri Synod	1,400	
Grand total	275,700	Congregational Church	600	
		Episcopalian-Free		
		Methodist, etc.	700	
		Adventists	23,000	
		Nazarenes	6,000	
			129,700	

Several conclusions leap out from these figures.

(1) Membership figures vary greatly. Table I shows
249,851 communicants, that is, full members. Table II shows
275,700. For the Presbyterians, Clyde Taylor in his 1961
Protestant Mission in Latin America, gives 66,000 — and this
is the figure Presbyterian missionaries in Mexico also give.
Gustavo Velasco gives 37,000 (or 43,000). The Executive

---

* The figures in column V are those of Gustavo Velasco; those in column T are from Clyde Taylor.

Secretary of the National Baptist Convention told us that
there were "at least 60,000 Baptists in Mexico," and he meant
full members. Taylor gives 15,000, without counting the Independent Baptists, the Conservative Baptists, and others.
Velasco gives 14,000 and 3,000 Independent Baptists in addition. Methodists in Taylor's report number 11,000 but Velasco
gives them 28,000 and the Independent Methodists 5,000 more.
The 1962 *World Christian Handbook* figures complicate the
issue still further.

Few churches or missions give undebatable figures. Ex-
ceptions are denominations with a conscience on membership
accounting. Gustavo Velasco's figures err, we believe, on the
conservative side. There are at least 275,700 communicant
Evangelicals. We would not quarrel with anyone who believed there were 350,000.

Christian missions should press on to a fully accurate
statement. It will take someone a year's work. It involves
both visiting each denominational's headquarters and inspect-
ing the rolls of some of its churches.

(2) Seven Pentecostal denominations have achieved memberships of 9,000 and above, whereas only three old-line denominations have done so.

(3) Five strong denominations of North America (Luth-
erans, American Baptists, Christian Churches, Congregation-
alists, and Episcopalians) have failed notably in "discipling
the Mexican nation." Though some of them work in resistant
populations, many of their mission stations are in responsive
populations, and yet their churches do not multiply.

(4) The tendency to break away from the North American denomination is very great in Mexico. There are independent or Mexican sections of each of the great denominations. The Pentecostals manifest this tendency as much as
the old-line denominations. There are two Assemblies of
God denominations, and the Independent Evangelical Pentecostals include a break away from the Swedish Pentecostals.

(5) These 1961 figures would be much more striking if
it were possible to draw a graph of the growth of each denom-

ination starting from zero and showing its membership at five-year intervals. The difference in size — now apparent — would be shown to have a close relationship to the difference in dynamism (potency). In general, the little Churches are not only little now — they have been little for a long time. Do they lack grace and power to make them successful in finding lost sheep?

We have no way of telling the amount of money from the United States which has gone into each of these denominations; but the common history of missions all around the world warrants the assumption that, whatever the sums, they will not correlate with the number of churches and members. Some missions with the least growth will have had large amounts of mission money, and those with the most growth will have had least. If money is regarded as a gross measure of effort — and it would seem reasonable to do this — we would probably have to affirm that effort has not been at all equally rewarded. This is part of the puzzle.

These two chapters — columns and tables — reinforce the picture of spotty and seemingly inconsistent growth. The rest of this book will be devoted to analysis of specific situations which illuminate the puzzle of church growth in Mexico and allow for proposed solutions and lead to conclusions and suggestions.

4 The Socio-Religious Mosaic

Part of the answer to the puzzle is found at once when we recognize that Mexico, like most lands, is not one homogeneous population, but is a mosaic made up of hundreds of separate populations or societies. There are, for example, 88 distinct Indian languages, grouped in eleven families of languages. That these have survived 400 years of Spanish domination means that these languages are spoken by 88 endogamous Indian tribes or societies — each separate from the other, as well as from the general population.

Many systems of classifying people are used. Some sociologists divide society into three main classes — upper, middle, and lower — and each of these again into three, as for example, the upper lower classes, the middle lower classes, and the lower lower classes.

We have chosen a different classification, one which takes into account factors bearing on church growth. The standard sociological classification mentioned above, for example, takes into account neither liberal nor conservative differences in Mexican society, nor the racial, tribal, and social elements which differentiate one group from another. For our purposes, then, we can profitably classify the hundreds of separate Mexican populations under ten broad headings. We shall speak of the "Ten Mexicos" in which 33 million Mexicans live.

The first Mexico is "Mexico City" itself. Here five million people from all over Mexico gather together in one of the great metropolises of the world. Life is anonymous. The pressures of the *rancho* (village) and the family are diminished. Travelers from all over the world meet there. Headquarters of many international organizations are there. The strait jacket in which the religious mind of Mexico has been kept so long is loosened and in some cases removed. In addition, many Mexicans are employed by government agencies and departments; and because the government is strongly secular, the Church of Rome is powerless to get Evangelicals fired from their jobs. Indeed, the Church of Rome finds it difficult to keep track of its own members, let alone to penalize, harass, or ostracize those who accept the biblical faith.

The second Mexico is the "Liberal Cities." Cities have character. One is liberal, another conservative. Monterrey and Torreon are counted liberal. So are the small cities of Sinaloa, Tamaulipas and the border states. Here the same influences found in the capital are at work, but in lesser measure. A smaller number of the people have jobs which cannot be touched by the priest of the Roman Catholic Church. Smaller numbers can resist the social pressures of families still ardently (though often ignorantly) Roman Catholic. In these cities, suburbs are being built — whole new developments of 200, 500, or 2,000 houses. People who move into them are receptive to the Gospel in a way in which those living in old residential sections of the cities with their hereditary homes and networks of relatives are not.

The "Conservative Cities" are the third Mexico. Guadalajara, Guanajuato, Aguascalientes, San Luis Potosi, Durango, and others fall into this category. For historic, geographic, social, and political reasons, these have shown themselves unresponsive to the Gospel. It is hard to get a hall in which to hold Evangelical services. Roman Catholic processions are organized against new Evangelical churches. It is hard to buy property for a church. Yet, even conservative cities today have their liberal and receptive sections. The new parts of the town are more receptive than the old.

The fourth Mexico is the "Tight Little Towns." These consist of a few hundred houses dominated by a huge church built many years ago, in some cases with state funds and forced labor. The population is a tight family web where everyone knows everyone else (and his grandfather, too).

Such towns resist the Evangel. Here control of the Church of Rome is super-effective and family loyalty and pressure is omnipresent. Towns in sections of the country such as Los Altos de Jalisco are more resistant than others. They have a more Iberian population, less immigration, and less liberalism. Evangelical churches get started in some of these towns and survive for decades with much mission aid (and sometimes with none) as little congregations of 10, 20, 40 or thereabouts.

The fifth Mexico is the "Roman Ranchos." In pre-revolutionary Mexico many, if not most, of the villages (*ranchos*) were located in large landed estates of colonial origin called *haciendas*. Other *ranchos* were separate from the *hacienda* with some of the villagers owning small plots of land and others working on some nearby *hacienda*. Still other *ranchos* were the vestiges of ancient Indian communities either independent in nature or tied to some *hacienda*. The Roman Catholic Church had a superb hold on all villages, either directly or indirectly through the *hacendado*, the large landholder. Today in *ranchos*, though political liberty has come, the religious feeling is still dominated by Roman Catholic sentiment. Response to the biblical faith is not great. Even when men from these *ranchos* go out to Mexico City, the United States, or the army, and get a liberal viewpoint, they dare not express it back home, and their children grow up in the old narrow tradition.

The sixth Mexico is the "Revolutionary Ranchos and Ejidos." When the Mexican Revolution began to distribute land, many villagers took sides with the government and fought side by side with federal troops to get the land from the *hacendados*. When the agrarian reform was finally implemented, these *agraristas* were among the first to get land. In some cases whole villages fought to get land and became the first *ejidos* (communal land holdings). The posture of the Roman Catholic Church towards agrarian reform instilled in these people a deep antipathy towards Rome. Since 1930 the government has created many new *ejidos,* some connected with vast new irrigation projects and others in newly cleared land. In these "Revolutionary Ranchos and Ejidos" responsiveness to the Gospel is potentially much greater than in the "Roman Ranchos," though even here family pressures, individual convictions, tradition, and spiritual apathy often prevent open espousal of the biblical faith.

Many Evangelical churches are in "Revolutionary Ranchos and Ejidos." Many leaders of *ejidos* are Evangelicals. In one village we visited, the pastor, himself landless, was active in pushing an application for 200 families (including his own) to be given land out of an undivided estate of 20,000 *hectares.* He was not sure whether he would be successful or not, for a well-connected landowner has means all along the line to delay distribution of his land and even to prevent it entirely. We heard of more than one land division which cost the lives of those pushing it. The "Revolutionary Rancho" may be indifferent to the Gospel, it may be communistic, it may even be Roman Catholic, but it is a far cry from the "Roman Rancho."

The seventh Mexico is the "Indian Tribes." Eighty-eight tribes have preserved enough of their blood and tribal separateness to have a language of their own. These victims of the Spanish conquest are often ardent Christo-pagans in the Roman Catholic tradition. They have their church buildings and their saints (their former gods). They give great allegiance to the various Virgins of their part of the country, especially the dark Virgin of Guadalupe!

Among Indians, people movements to Christ, quite similar to people movements in tribal populations everywhere, are possible. Till such a people movement begins, the tight social structure and aloofness of the Indian operate to make "Indian work" a rather fruitless labor for Protestants. But when a people movement to Christ begins — as it has among a number of tribes — many persons in groups of families are won for Christ and formed into solid Evangelical churches.

Part of the great growth of the Protestant Church in Mexico comes from these people movements in the Indian tribes.[1]

The eighth Mexico is "Tabasco." This province in the hook of Mexico is in a class by itself. Its story will be told in Chapter 8. Twelve thousand of its population are members in Evangelical Churches. The Protestant community numbers at least 40,000, which is a tenth of the total population.

The ninth Mexico is the "Northern Border Country," particularly the border towns. Here there is constant movement to and from the United States. The influence of the free land, where religious liberty is an accomplished fact and the Roman Catholic Church does not attempt extra-religious pressures, is felt in the border country in many ways. The evils of America also flow across the border, and the race prejudice of "the Anglos" alienates some Mexicans. Religious indifference is considerable. But Protestant churches have prospered in the border country, and nothing creates a responsiveness better than living, multiplying churches. The Methodist Church has profited by the 1917 comity agreement which gave it the Border Country — though the Congregational Church in equally responsive Sinaloa and Sonora has not. Some denominations which do not observe comity have also done well in the border land.

The tenth Mexico we call "Oscar's Masses." We refer, of course, to Oscar Lewis, who has described in pitiful and pitiless detail the hopeless life of the poverty-stricken urban masses. Some turn with disgust from his descriptions, but he is a competent anthropologist.[2]

City masses are a common feature of human society in all lands and all ages, and the Christian who reads the first chapter of First Corinthians remembers that, again and again,

1 Anyone working among Indians should read *Bridges of God* by McGavran, and *Church Growth in the High Andes* by Hamilton.
2 Oscar Lewis, *Five Families* — Mexican Case Studies in the Culture of Poverty (Basic Books).

vital Christianity has redeemed just such masses. In some denominations in Mexico, Brazil, and other lands, he meets many redeemed men and women of the masses. The future belongs to the common people; and if these, in the day of their dire need, turn to Christ, they and their children will be His when, after an arduous march, they reach Canaan. "Oscar's Masses" are an important part of the Mexican Mosaic, and Evangelical Churches should pay more attention to them.

These Ten Mexicos were much more alike a hundred years ago. Diversity is growing. Ten years from now they will be still more different in their response to the Christian Gospel. That Christian mission is being carried out in a rapidly changing social order is a truism. What is not often recognized is that this rapid change influences receptivity and hence is important to church growth.

The Church of Christ has a different opportunity to grow in each of the Ten Mexicos. One of the reasons for large growth in one state and not in another, and in one city and not in another, is this: growth of the Evangelical Church in each of the Ten Mexicos proceeds at a different rate.

Effective *discipling*[3] in the Ten Mexicos requires keeping abreast of changes in responsiveness in each section. It is not sufficient to prepare missionaries for Mexico or Latin America. The missionary, and even more the national minister, must be prepared to recognize which Mexico he is in and *what kind of presentation* in *it* is actually blessed by the Holy Spirit to the increase of the Church.

Great growth has occurred in some sections of Mexico.

3 Discipling. The revelation of God, as given in Christ and the New Testament, requires that the Church, to be the Church (i.e. the body of Christ) should be enormously concerned that all men know, love and obey the Saviour. This means that winning persons to Christ and responsible membership in His multiplying churches is an integral part of all churchhood. Effective discipling of persons, groups, and eventually large populations is therefore essential.

Once varying responsiveness is recognized as a legitimate basis for emphasis in Christian mission, there will be still greater growth where growth can take place.

5 Elements Making for Static Churches

Anyone who would understand church growth in Mexico must see not only the ten Mexicos, but also those elements, internal and external, which arrest the multiplication of churches. The external elements are intense Roman Catholic opposition and the chaos of war and revolution.

About the first, little needs to be said. The Roman Catholic Church stamped out the Reformation in Spain and resolved that Spanish possessions (Latin America and the Philippines) should be hermetically sealed against "the wicked and disastrous heresy." Protestants were literally barred from entry. The Inquisition ruled in Mexico for two hundred years and made sure that any who stole their way into Mexico were ferreted out and killed. As the power of the Inquisition weakened, a few Protestants did come in. At first they could not be buried in cemeteries nor could they build churches in which to worship. Later, when Protestant churches were built, they were often burned. The feeling of the ignorant masses and of the classes was one of superstitious and fanatical opposition to any variety of biblical faith. Innumerable instances could be recounted. For example, when the first Evangelical lady in Villahermosa, Tabasco, had a baby, a Roman Catholic woman ran through the streets shouting that the *Protestante* baby had been born with horns and a tail!

The chaos of war and revolution also slowed down the growth of the churches. From 1910 to 1918 armies marched. Passions burned hot. Anti-Americanism, fomented by oil imperialism and punitive expeditions into Mexico, brought about frequent flares of anti-missionary feeling. In 1914 missionaries felt they had to leave the country and could not come back for several years. In its desperate attempts to free itself from the domination of the foreign Roman Catholic hierarchy, the government of Mexico passed laws which seemed to damage Protestant missions. After the agrarian revolution, the anti-clerical and anti-religion parties made it difficult for the Protestants in several provinces, notably Tabasco, where all priests and ministers were barred from the state. Church services were not allowed. Images of saints were ordered buried and Bibles were ordered burned. The drive to free the State from Roman Catholic domination placed all education in the hands of the State and led some missionaries to close their schools. Since others remained open, closure may not have been really necessary.

Only since 1935 has there been that widespread civil peace which allows regular, orderly work. In the disturbed times before 1935, therefore, some Evangelical Churches grew slowly and with many setbacks. Some, however, prospered. Contrasting the two yields some insights into the nature of church growth.

Internal elements also slowed down growth.

The closeness to the United States and the ease with which missionaries could come into Mexico often resulted in two or more Evangelical denominations working in the same towns and cities. Free competition, which has marked the various Branches of the Church of Christ in North America, marked missions in Mexico. Despite nine missions agreeing in 1917 to work according to comity, competition continued. Five large missions stayed out of comity. So did national Churches and later missions from North America, such as the Pentecostals and Churches of God.

It is often asserted that competition slowed down the Evangelical movement; yet it must be granted that the most rapidly growing Churches in Mexico, which are blazing a trail for all Evangelicals and softening up the opposition in innumerable places, would never have had their wide influence if they had allowed the comity system to limit their field.

Indeed, some observers maintain that the Cincinnati Plan, by which the 1917 comity assignments were made, was really detrimental to the Protestant cause. It jolted all missions badly, severing them from some of their churches. It divided Evangelicals into Co-operators and Intruders. It proceeded on the erroneous assumption that one mission board would do all that could possibly be done in a vast population. Had comity been strictly observed, the Congregational Church, with about 300 members in 9 small, static churches (1962 figures), would today be the only Protestant force in 800-mile-long Sinaloa, an increasingly responsive state.

Another internal obstacle to growth was that, faced with high resistance, some missions turned to the "mission station approach." The process was this. When converts, who were few and far between, constantly faced stone, torch and gun from the Roman Catholic Church, Evangelicals were driven to gradualism. They undertook not direct conversion but enterprises "which did something else now so that the Evangelical Church could grow later on." A missionary in the twenties and thirties describing the work of his mission wrote, "We have wonderful opportunities to have warm, personal relationships with the outstanding business and professional people of the city. Our school opens the door for friendship with wonderful people." Gradualism may have been necessary in some cases, but a gradualistic enterprise, once established, has a habit of continuing long after it is unnecessary.

In the same way some missions retreated into service institutions. "If they will not hear the Gospel and obey Christ's call, let us serve them lovingly." "If the government will not let us preach, let us minister quietly in the name of Christ." The dream of influencing the educated classes, already so violently anti-clerical in many parts of Latin America, led to the establishment of schools. That these did good work none can doubt. They lifted Evangelical boys and girls out of the masses and started them into the middle classes. They also gave large numbers of Roman Catholics a good Christian education. But they did not multiply churches.

Small congregations, facing a hostile multitude and existing as an encircled community, turned in upon themselves. Evangelical youth married Evangelical youth (though not as often as might be desired) and the Evangelicals became a community separated more and more from the Roman Catholics. The second generation was more separated than the first.

In the mission-station approach, the union of "mission good works" with "family churches" proved low in reproductive capacity. Converts were won, but not in large enough numbers to push Evangelical churches out into the main stream of the population.

Another internal element which led to non-growing churches was the precarious position of an exposed minority. Protestant standards were high. Ministers and missionaries were preaching that faith in Christ redeems personally and socially. Those who backslid into man or woman trouble, drink, or worldliness, dropped out of the church. They seldom went back to Rome. They were just "lost to the world." Losses also took place to Rome through marriage. Small Evangelical groups have even smaller numbers of adolescent boys and girls. When these get married to Roman Catholics, sometimes the partner becomes an Evangelical; but often the Evangelical becomes a Roman Catholic. Fervent denominations have low losses through marriage. The less fervent have high losses. Other losses take place when young people from the very small Protestant minority move from *ranchos* to the city. They may find and unite with a church, but often they are lost.

Where these three kinds of losses are larger than the gains by evangelism, there the church stagnates. A sealed-off mentality develops. A brave little band of 15 to 50 Christians remains. These Christians hang onto their faith and their church, but they do not do much evangelism. Little churches characterize many towns, *pueblos,* and *ranchos,* especially in some states and denominations. Sometimes these churches die, but more often they struggle on bravely for years.

Where mission institutions are found, there the sealed-off church often grows to a membership of 80, 100, or even 200. The institutions give prestige to the church and education, fellowship, and encouragement to the young Evangelicals. But mission station churches seldom multiply. Their members often are educated men and women and firm Evangelicals. They gain by biological growth (their children grow up as Evangelicals) and by an occasional conversion. They lose when their members move or lapse to the world. Because some of their children marry Roman Catholics, a number of half families are commonly found. Because they want to get along with their neighbors, they hesitate to be aggressively evangelistic. Some have paid a high price for their faith and believe it is well to be careful.

Furthermore, near institutions a curious condition is commonly found which inhibits growth. Members of the institutional staff (nationals and missionaries) come to know each other extremely well. Their conversation is inevitably about mutual interests, problems, equipment, undertakings, friends, students, patients, and employees. This is their world. Staff members always go to church and often comprise its leadership. Observe them coming out of church, and you will see them and hear them moving inside their own world. A potential convert approaches any church timidly, sits on the back seats, hesitates to find or sing unfamiliar hymns, and follows the service with difficulty. After church he hurries out and away as fast as he can. Often he goes away without anyone speaking to him. But even if active Christians make it a point to speak to him and introduce him to several, there is little to talk about because he is not of their world. This is especially the case if he is a country man.

The more Christian the church, the more love it manifests among the members, the more they are truly one family, the more difficult it is for newcomers to become a real part of its specialized world. Indeed, the only way old Christians (missionaries and members) of a friendly institutional church can become evangelistically potent is to give enough time and prayer to personal evangelism so that considerable numbers of outside persons become a part of their world. About these persons they converse — and pray — frequently. When such persons come to church, the old Christians welcome them, sit with them, make them feel at home in the service, and after worship talk easily to *them* rather than to old friends!

Another element causing some churches to be static is their national leadership. One frequently hears it said that a cure for a static church is to turn it over to the nationals, but this is not necessarily true. Whether the leaders' mother tongue is English or Spanish, they all face the same conditions, the same encirclement, the same impenetrable barrier of a friendly family. Just as one generation of missionaries can transmit low expectations and gradualistic techniques to their successor missionaries, so can they to their successor nationals. In general, if a Church was growing before control passed to nationals, it will continue growing under them. If it was not growing, it will continue static. Both nationals and missionaries, therefore, should learn all they can about church growth and practice all they learn.

Another potent element making for little growth in Mexico is the Shadow of the North. Denominations in the United States, facing the situation there, develop a way of life which enables their congregations to survive and grow. This way is unconsciously followed by their church members and is taught in their seminaries. Missionaries then come to Mexico with these "denominational ways of doing things," which we call "cultural overhangs." Some overhangs are highly detrimental to the multiplication of churches in Mexico. Let us look at two examples.

In North America, nominal church membership is often substituted for a personal experience of Christ. For example, I once had neighbors who said they were Methodists. They had not gone to church in twenty years and contributed nothing to it; but they had been baptized and married in that church and had sent their children to its Sunday School. They were, in fact, members not of any church but of "the Protestant World." I proposed to my minister that we put this couple on our prayer list and try to win them for Christ through our fellowship of earnest Christians. "No," he replied, "that would be sheep stealing." When, through cultural overhang, this minister's North American attitude is carried to Mexico and an Evangelical Church begins to regard imparting Christ to multitudes of "the Roman Catholic World" as sheep stealing, it is doomed to a sickly existence.

A Church in North America calls itself a New Testament Church — a name of prestige there in a Bible-knowing population. Because of cultural overhang, missionaries of this denomination think the name will have equal prestige in Mexico. But this name does not attract men of the Spanish civilization. They have not been accustomed to regard the New Testament as authority. They would be more favorably impressed by a name such as "The Holy Apostolic Church of Christ."

A final internal factor which inhibits church growth is a low view of the Church, a view where open confession of Christ followed by responsible membership in His Church is not that for which we should immediately labor. The low view of the Church adopts things other than church membership as the primary goal of mission.

In Mexico a low view develops easily. A typical process is described below. For three hundred years the Roman Catholic Church implanted in all Mexicans an intense repugnance to the thought of "becoming Protestants." The Inquisition burned "heretics, sorcerers, bigamists, and protestants." The very word "Protestant" was despised. Till late in the nineteenth century, the establishment of an Evangelical Church by Mexicans was not only impossible, but the thought itself would have been rejected as vile.

Under these circumstances, missionaries of the true, apostolic, catholic and biblical faith found that a chief way to open the closed citadel of the people's mind was to place in men's hands a copy of the Bible. The Bible was beyond question the Authoritative Scripture of the Roman Catholic Church. The person beginning to read it did not imagine he could become a hated Protestant. He was simply reading his own authoritative Bible. When the priest or bishop took it away from him and burned it, he felt his private rights invaded. He often hid it, read it in secret, and pondered why the Roman Catholic Church had distorted apostolic doctrines so greatly and departed from them so thoroughly.

Of the thousands who read the Bible in secret — knowing it was forbidden by the hierarchy — hundreds were gradually convinced that the true biblical faith was something other than Roman Catholicism. Scores had the courage and opportunity to become Protestants. These self-convinced, highly intelligent, and Bible-believing converts were the sure foundation of many a pioneer Protestant congregation. Stories of ways in which the Bible led to Evangelical Faith are found in all accounts of the beginning of the Church of Christ in Mexico.

Since reading the Bible was a chief and sometimes the only way to conversion, the distribution of the Scriptures assumed a place of enormous importance in missionary thinking. Getting a person to "read the Bible" was the goal. Even after 1900 — when Bibles and New Testaments could be sold and distributed without too much danger — a person who would "read the Bible" was considered well on the way to a saving faith in Christ.

G. B. Winton, in *Mexico Today,* says, "That Book is the ally of all intellectual and social struggles after better things. It arouses the minds of those who touch it for the first time as nothing else will and profoundly stirs the moral conscience. It makes men demand enlightenment. It is the mother of the public school. It is the enemy of darkness. It inspires courage. It drives the human mind to test and investigate. By thrusting final responsibility on the individual heart and brain, it is in particular the enemy of a religion which habitually delegates authority and demands submission."

To get people to "read the Bible" was so desirable an end that it sometimes eclipsed the supreme need for their becoming responsible members of the Church of Christ and establishing churches. People who read the Bible but could not (or did not) actually unite with the church were a source of comfort and consolation to many a minister and missionary. Thus all across Latin America a category of persons is commonly recognized — the sympathizers. These are Bible readers, liberals and anti-clericals who believe on Christ, and other near-converts, who, for one reason and another, do not openly unite with the church.

To the extent that Bible reading, confession of Christ, or other preparatory acts are accepted in lieu of membership as a goal of Christian mission, a low view of the Church prevails. The "low view" says, "It is enough now to read the Bible — or to believe on Christ. Later, perhaps, membership in our church will come."

This form of gradualism — like all gradualism — is justified when membership in the living Church is truly impossible. Grave danger exists, however, that this limited goal will be sought long after membership and church multiplication have become possible. Any denomination or Christian stopping with preparatory acts when others in the same city or countryside are planting churches has a low view of the Church and is engaging in unjustifiable gradualism.

In contrast, a high view of the Church — held by all growing churches in Mexico — shows how the Bible teaches that salvation is to those who believe on Jesus Christ, who become responsible members of an Evangelical Branch of His Church, and who engage in further church multiplication.

6 Elements Making for Growing Churches

Above all elements making for church growth stands the Founder of the Church, Jesus Christ our Lord. The Indwelling Christ redeems believers and adds them to the assemblies of God. He it is who makes them a new creation, who calls them (not many wise, not many noble, things that are not) and makes them shame the wise and the strong, and put down things that are. It is He who marshals and disciplines and multiplies His churches and sends them out conquering and to conquer. Jesus Christ, King of Kings and Lord of Lords, shows believers how to use elements which make churches grow. The Holy Spirit equips Christians to carry out His will and disciple the nations.

No skillful use of the elements described below without fervent discipleship, abundant prayer, and joyful surrender to Him who died for us will "produce" church growth. But with Christ dwelling in the heart through faith, wills kept in harmony with His, and overflowing gratitude to Him for His amazing love, denominations and congregations exhibiting and using the elements described are growing and will grow.

Seven tremendous new elements have created and will continue to create a new responsiveness to the Evangelical Faith. They help make churches grow. Three of these may be termed *environmental elements*. They are created by governments, economic forces, the spread of science, and the birth of a new world. Four of them are *spiritual elements*. They are created specifically by the churches or the missions. In varying degrees, both environmental and spiritual elements play on each of the Ten Mexicos and all their people and make for more or less church growth.

52

First comes protection offered by a secular government increasingly aware of world opinion and convinced that the function of government in a pluralistic society is to protect all religions and favor none.

The revolutionary implications of this secular stand can best be seen against the traditional stand of the Roman Catholic Church. In April, 1948, the official world organ of the Jesuits, *Civalta Cattolica,* of Rome, published the following lucid statement about the function of government toward religious minorities where the majority of the population is Roman Catholic. It said, "The Roman Catholic Church, convinced through its divine prerogatives of being the only true Church, must demand the right of freedom for herself alone. As to other religions, the Church will certainly never draw the sword, but she will require that by legitimate means they shall not be allowed to propagate false doctrines. Consequently, in a state where the majority of the people are Catholic, the Church will require that legal existence be denied to error, and that if religious minorities actually exist, they shall have only a *de facto* existence, without opportunity to spread their beliefs. . . . In some countries Catholics will be obliged to ask full religious freedom for all, resigned at being forced to cohabitate where they alone should rightfully be allowed to live. But in doing this the Church does not renounce her thesis, which remains the most imperative of her laws, but merely adapts herself to *de facto* conditions, which must be taken into account in practical affairs. . . . The Church cannot blush for her own want of tolerance, as she asserts it in principle and applies it in practice."[1]

Naturally, the stand of the secular government is abhorrent to the Roman Catholic Church and to ardent Roman Catholics. "Protecting all religions and favoring none" is

1 In 1963, one dares hope that the Roman Catholic Church will soon, on a world-wide scale, declare for genuine freedom of conscience, and thus officially deny this Jesuit statement. But until such pronouncement is made and implemented, the protection offered by a secular government will remain a potent factor.

not their idea of the duty of the government. Yet the secular state is well entrenched in Mexico, both in the constitution and in the hearts of the people. "Roman Catholic" Mexicans vote for the secular government. Recently, the State of Aguascalientes elected a governor. The government candidate won by 38,000 to 3000 votes. Protection offered by a secular government is a potent environmental factor in the growth of Evangelical churches.

To be sure, until the Pope and the bishops discipline priests for harassing converts and inciting the faithful to oppress Evangelicals, dominantly Roman Catholic sections of the country will — despite the constitution — find ways to persecute Evangelicals. But in serious persecution, government sides with the Evangelical. Church buildings are government property. Once a property has been purchased and given to the government as a church, any action against it is an action against government property. Government defends its own property.

The protection of a secular government is increasing with the passage of the years. For example, in 1938 a band of believers in Tabasco had their house burned over their heads. They then built a church, and on the day it was completed the Roman Catholics burned it. In neither case did they get any protection from the government. But in 1962 the Baptists in Durango built a new church, and when it was stoned and the windows broken, government moved swiftly to rebuke those who thus damaged the reputation of Mexico.

In many cities Evangelical churches have much glass in their doors and windows. They do not suffer attack — they are government property. In Pabellon, Aguascalientes, when the church was built in 1954, a fanatical group of Roman Catholic women, who had previously threatened a missionary with violence if he did not leave town, molested the worshipers at the communion service. The opposition continued to grow. On a later Sunday evening, hundreds, including armed men, gathered near the church, intending violence. An army colonel in command of a detachment of soldiers dispersed the crowd and sent soldiers for several weeks after that to guard the Evangelical church during its services. He also rebuked the women who had created the disturbance.

The top leadership of the Roman Catholic Church, too, has begun to follow a more Christian course and some priests are saying to their congregations, "The Evangelicals are good people. You might emulate some of their good qualities. Do not trouble them."

The days of fanatical reprisal, stoning, processions, and threatening Evangelicals with death are not over in some sections of Mexico, but government protection, on the one hand, and a change of the form of Roman Catholic opposition on the other, does favor growth of Evangelical churches. To sum it all up, we may say that, although we must limit and condition "government protection of all religions," a neutral government dedicated to protecting all faiths greatly favors responsiveness.

The second environmental element is the tremendous growth of the secular world. The current of world affairs flows through Mexico. A considerable body of citizens has been influenced by Marxist ideology, positivist philosophy, and the relativism of the modern world. Masonry, trade unionism, anti-clericalism and rationalism are well known. Many leaders of the Social Revolution were — and are — out and out secularists. The same influences which make for a materialistic, secularistic outlook on life in North America operate in Mexico.

As soon as Mexicans get away from Mexico, most of them quit going to mass. It is estimated that of the two million Latins in Texas, 85 percent do not attend mass or any worship service of God at all.

Secularization of life moves unequally in the various strata of society, but it flows freely in most. Manufacturing complexes, electrified cities, irrigation systems, and modern transportation all give man the feeling that God is no longer necessary.

In the past, the Church of Rome has kept the secular

world under tight rein, but today no Church holds its nominal members under tight rein. Tomorrow it will control them still less. Thus the Evangelical Churches in Mexico live in the dawn of a day when these secularized blocks of people, increasing decade by decade, introduce a new element in church growth. "We find the bulk of the population indifferent to the Gospel," said some of our informants. Winning secularists is different from winning Roman Catholics. No one should be naive enough to believe that secularists are easily persuaded to become disciples of Christ; yet the growth of the secular world and the increasing pluralism of the Mexican population does make it much more possible for people to hear, believe, and follow Christ as revealed in biblical faith.

The third favorable environmental element in Evangelical growth is the working-class people who travel to the United States and back into Mexico. This has been going on for many years, and literally millions have been involved. Again and again some family, church, or cluster of churches traces its beginning to a man who went to the United States and was there influenced toward the Holy Faith of Jesus Christ and His apostles, or even converted and baptized.

Had Christians in the United States regarded each Mexican laborer they met as a man for whom Christ died, whom it was their high privilege to bring to salvation, Mexico by now might have been largely Evangelical. By and large, however, Christians in America were stopped by their inability to speak or understand Spanish and by their lack of evangelistic passion for Mexican laborers. Multitudes of Mexican laborers returned to Mexico without becoming acquainted with the Lord of Life and the Bible. But here and there the light did shine. Spanish New Testaments were distributed to "Mexican labor." Mexicans were taken to church and invited to homes to eat. They heard the Gospel in their own language. They saw a Protestant land. They worked for Protestant farmers. They realized that what they had been told about Evangelicals was a lie. Evangelicals were good people. Above all, Christ became more to them than a dead figure on a cross. He became the Power of God enabling believers to live new, victorious lives.

There are over three million Mexicans now living permanently in the United States as citizens. Other Mexicans reside in the United States for long periods without becoming citizens. These men and their families are "the Mexicans" known by most Americans. These are the "migrants" for whom "home missions" carries on such a large program of care. Some of these are becoming Protestants — by several different paths. People in Mexico hear that their relatives have become Evangelicals. "My daughters in Los Angeles have become Evangelicals. They sent me a New Testament. I read it and became an Evangelical with the rest of my family here," said a new convert to us.

High wages in the United States lead many Mexicans to slip illegally across the border and return home after making much money. Because these cross the border by swimming the Rio Grande, they are called "wet-backs." Although border guards have been multiplied, and it is now much more difficult to get into the United States this way, many still come and go. Each of these is a potential convert.

During World War II, large numbers of Mexican men were employed in the United States, with the consent of both governments. They were recruited in Mexico, taken to the United States, housed in barracks, fed and treated according to strict regulations, and returned to Mexico. This came to be known as the *bracero* program. Between 1946 and 1962, from 200,000 to 500,000 men a year were legally taken in and sent back. Their earnings amounted to hundreds of millions of dollars. This became one of Mexico's chief ways of earning dollars.

While in the United States, some *braceros* never saw any Evangelicals. In other cases, Evangelicals came to their barracks, entertained them, preached the Gospel and gave them Bibles and New Testaments. In such meetings, some *braceros* made decisions for Christ. Sometimes priests circu-

lated through the camps telling the men to beware of Protestants. One man said to us, "A Roman Catholic priest came
and told us to tear up our Bibles. We did so, but I kept
my New Testament. I read it, but did not become an Evangelical. Years later, however, when the Gospel was preached
in my *rancho,* I accepted Christ and was baptized."

This element in church growth does not operate auto-
matically. Some denominations have never found the *braceros.* One church in Mexico, located on the edge of one of the
bracero shipping stations, in the midst of thousands of men
milling around waiting for orders to move, has never distributed tracts, put on a movie to bring men in and preach the
gospel to them afterward, or set up a social center where the
men could find wholesome entertainment and the truth about
Christ. But other denominations have sought out the *braceros,* both in Mexico and the United States. Pentecostal
churches, being churches of the common man, have found
much *bracero* responsiveness. They have communicated
Christ to Mexican laborers in the United States, and they
have won many people of the working classes in Mexico.

The leaven of the "America-returned" is widespread in
Mexico. Men from both resistant sections and receptive sections return influenced — a few converted, some friendly to
Evangelicals, some having read the New Testament, and some
merely jarred a little in their age-long prejudices. This leaven
is an important element in Evangelical growth.

The first of the spiritual elements creating responsiveness
to Evangelical Christianity is apostolic faith. Apostolic Evangelical faith marks growing churches in Mexico. It is espoused because of its reasonableness. What the apostles obviously believed, did, and commanded, that the Evangelical
Church in varying measure does. Once a Mexican has studied
the Bible and seen what the Church of Jesus Christ and
His holy apostles really is, he seldom reverts to Rome. He
believes the Gospel in the same way that he believes the
multiplication tables. It is obviously and inescapably true.
There is no circumlocution to show that, while the Bible

says this, the Church is justified in doing that. The simplicity, directness, and sweet reasonableness of the Apostolic Evangelical faith wins its way into the hearts of men.

Evangelical faith in Mexico has an amazing vitality. It grows and reproduces. Driven underground in many places, it has multiplied. Persecuted, it has increased. When in Tabasco, Governor Canabal ordered Romanists to bury their saints and Evangelicals to burn their Bibles, one of his Evangelical employees sturdily replied, "The Governor has purchased my labor. I will serve him faithfully and obediently in all things. But he has not purchased my conscience. I will not burn my Bible." Men converted in the United States or in Mexico City have gone back to their *ranchos* and started churches. That this has taken place so rarely in some states is a testimony to Roman Catholic oppression; that it has taken place often in others is a testimony to Evangelical vitality.

Tough, reasonable Evangelical faith has exerted a constant evangelistic pressure on its surroundings — much greater than the evangelistic pressure exerted by the average congregation in the United States. Evangelism has been diminished here and there in Mexico by church and mission policies, such as entrenched gradualism and neutral good works. Some congregations also have become sealed off and have turned in on themselves. They exist as happy families of Christians without "preaching the word." But they are not typical. The typical congregation believes itself entrusted with the biblical faith which it must proclaim.

A correct statement of this first spiritual element uses the words "an apostolic faith" or "an apostolic biblical faith." Some other phrases we have used betray our cultural overhang. The North American Christian speaks of a "tough, reasonable Evangelical faith." That appeals to secularized North America. It does not appeal to people in a Roman Catholicized Mexican culture. In that, what gives a faith supreme value is that it is the faith of Jesus Christ and His Holy Apostles; it is apostolic. What the Bible says the apostles believed and taught, that the Evangelicals believe and teach. "Simply read and see."

The second spiritual or missionary element making for growing churches is the penetration of society by Evangelical radio, correspondence courses, and newspaper articles. Evangelical radio reaches behind the velvet curtain with which the Church of Rome guards her people from Biblical truth. Many Roman Catholics listen to Evangelical radio and like what they hear. A pastor in Costa Rica told me of passing a house on which was pasted a card, "Protestants Stay Out," and hearing through the window the sweet music of a hymn being broadcast by the Latin America Mission Radio. Evangelical radio is, of course, of varied quality. But much of it is interesting and true. There is usually a positive, courteous, and reasonable presentation of the Gospel. People in general like Evangelical radio. Through it a new image of Evangelicalism is being created all across Latin America.

Correspondence courses carried out by Presbyterians, Adventists, and others enroll large numbers. A few become responsible members of Evangelical churches. A much greater proportion believes the Biblical position is the truth, and yet they lack courage openly to become Evangelicals. Scores of thousands of such ex-students are now to be found in Mexico. They are frequently responsive to the Gospel when they hear it later on presented by some other denomination.

A blind Adventist preacher in one of the resistant cities of the Meseta Central illustrates the effect of radio and correspondence courses. He said:

> My church of 48 members in this city and 78 in the entire state, represents 32 years of work. Our temple was erected 18 years ago. We have had 14 converts in the past 3 years. I visit 40 people systematically — 25 Roman Catholics and 15 who have had some connection with the Gospel. We are growing in recent years more than before. Even in this resistant part of the country, there is more response. We Adventists have 11 radio broadcasts a day, to which many people listen. We also

have a correspondence course, which many people take. Six of our 14 converts came from those who took the correspondence course. I have the names of 55 persons in this state taking our correspondence course. They have my address, too. I have visited 22 of the 55. Last year 2500 men and women joined the Seventh-Day Adventist Church through studying our correspondence course.

If the Adventists in Mexico gained 2500 converts, we may be sure that 25,000 took the course in part or whole, liked what they read of the Bible, and began to recognize that apostolic Christianity was more like Evangelical Faith than like Roman Catholicism.

Radio and correspondence courses decrease prejudice and increase receptivity, even though few conversions come directly from them. When followed up by personal visits and instruction, they often bring conviction and baptism. There is a good deal of transfer, too. A man said, "I heard the Adventists' radio and became curious. So I went to the nearest Evangelical Church (Baptist) and was converted."

Newspaper articles are constantly read. North American magazines in translation circulate freely — though some of these are fairly well Roman Catholicized. Occasionally Evangelicals buy newspaper space and put in an Evangelical article as an advertisement. These also are read. The English-reading section of the Mexican public reads the cosmopolitan pluralistic views of Europe and America. Much interest in the Evangelical Faith has been begun or intensified by reading, radio, or correspondence courses — unknown thirty years ago.

The third tremendous spiritual element is the large increase of Evangelicals in Mexico. This is not 1917 when missions could parcel out huge sections of Mexico and consider each "well occupied" with one missionary per 200,000 people and one beleaguered church building in the state capital. This is 1962 when Evangelical membership is increasing rapidly.

Today Evangelical communicants in Mexico number a quarter of a million, their community a half a million, and the Evangelical world — in which we include sympathizers and lapsed, cold Evangelicals, or people of Evangelical parentage — at least a million. Evangelicals are not evenly distributed. One in forty in Mexico City is said to be an Evangelical; but only one in a thousand in Guanajuato. Yet they are all in Mexico. They are all Mexican citizens. They are sometimes elected to high office. Some are among the best citizens. Multitudes are humble laborers and peasants.

The denominationalism of North America, the lack of ecumenicity even among the ecumenicals, and the rift between conservatives and liberals obscures this tremendous spiritual element. One wing tends to minimize "Pentecostal progress" — until it visits many churches of a tithing, self-supporting and self-respecting Pentecostal denomination. The other wing tends to minimize the progress of the old-line denominations — until it sees the spread of truely Christian churches in Tabasco, Chiapas, and other states. Presbyterians, Apostolics, Baptists, Holiness, Methodists, Pentecostals, Congregationals, Adventists, Nazarenes, Churches of God — these are all allies, whether they realize it or not. When all are added together, there are quite a lot of us!

Mexico has seen large growth of indigenous Branches of the Church of Christ. Without calling it such, they have followed the Pauline method of missions described by the Anglican Roland Allen.[2] Their unconscious missionary methods are these: Each Christian is a missionary. Each group of Christians (local church) is left largely to the guidance of the Holy Spirit and the Scriptures — as were the churches in the first century. The missionary who starts a church does not stay for years to serve, govern and guide it but hurries on to plant other churches. Qualifications for the ministry are primarily spiritual and not educational.

2 *Missionary Methods: St. Paul's or Ours* by Roland Allen (Wm. B. Eerdmans Publishing Co., 1962).

Ministers are trained in service or are given short courses; they are primarily laymen, competent to earn a living in some other way and accustomed to do it even while pastoring a church. Thus new little churches find pastors among themselves of people like themselves, supported at about their level, and happy to earn part of their living by "making tents."

This sort of church is able to reproduce indefinitely. Not dependent on foreign money or personnel, it grows even when foreigners are banned. In Tabasco, in several Indian tribes, in Mexico City, and along the border, such indigenous churches have multiplied.

The extension of indigenous churches has increased responsiveness. Extension of any Evangelical Church helps all the rest. When the Methodists gain a hundred thousand, it will be a glad day for both Mexico and all other Evangelicals. Despite an occasional "gift" of members from one denomination to another (which always is hard for the losing church to bear), all Evangelical Churches — indigenous and old-line — are essentially allies. At a Disciples Church, a laywoman was explaining a chapter in Acts with great fervor and good sense to a group going out to evangelize a responsive *rancho*. "She is one of our most enthusiastic workers," said the pastor, "a former Pentecostal converted straight out of the world." In another field, new Congregational converts had been greatly influenced by the Apostolics and were among the most vigorous of the Christians. A potent element in Evangelical growth is a mighty spread of indigenous — and other — Churches.

The great increase in Evangelicals has created an "Evangelical World." There are in Mexico hundreds of thousands of people whose parents were Evangelicals or who came from families where one parent was an Evangelical. Many of these are themselves *nada*. Their prediliction is toward the Evangelical Faith. In the general population are millions of close relatives of sound Evangelicals, fervent Methodists, reborn Baptists, devoted Pentecostals, convinced Presbyterians

— in short, changed Christians. Some of these "Roman Catholic" relatives are in reality part of the Evangelical World. They say, "It is good for my cousins to become Evangelicals. Protestantism makes for progress. Some day we'll be Evangelicals, too."

Nothing increases general responsiveness like the spread of Evangelical churches. Every Christian has scores of relatives who know him intimately. Every congregation is a center of influence. Even weak Christians and weak congregations are more influential than we suppose, for they have far more contacts than any foreign missionary can possibly have. The great increase of Evangelicals today creates an entirely new magnitude of responsiveness. To see the changed situation, one has only to compare today with 1890 or even 1930.

The heightened expectations of Evangelical churches is a fourth tremendous spiritual element making for church growth.

The missions in Mexico, which between 1880 and 1940 met with scant response, great persecution, and terrible prejudice, learned by bitter experience to cultivate low expectations. Roman Catholic Mexico was, they believed, almost an Islamic land. But the curve of Evangelical church growth in Mexico shows a rocket-like upsurge in the last 20 years. Today only "out-of-date people," as a minister called them, think the Church cannot grow in Mexico. "We grew from 65 members in 1958 to 135 in 1962," said the same minister, "and when we get to 200 we shall divide this church into two and each will grow vigorously." This certainty of future growth was, to be sure, in one of the more receptive Mexicos, but it speaks prophetically.

A minister in a resistant highland city pointed out a new congregation with forty members established in one year: twenty members were a gift from an existing church and twenty members were new. A missionary told of a new congregation with 27 baptized members which had been established in Mexico City among oil workers after a five-day meeting. He assured us that the same thing could be repeated in many sections of the city many times a year. He was planning to establish 200 churches in Mexico City in the next twenty years at the rate of ten a year. Will they be planted? We do not know. We are speaking of heightened expectations. No such plan would have occurred to anyone of any denomination in 1930. His heightened expectations are symptomatic of the new day and are an essential element in church growth. If Evangelical leaders face today's open doors with yesterday's expectations, not much church growth will occur. But if they can unite opportunity with heightened expectations, God will grant them growth as they have faith.

Any understanding of the church growth situation in Mexico must be vividly conscious of these elements. Any judgment as to the future course of Christian mission must estimate how responsive Mexico is going to be in the next twenty years. Men attempt what they believe possible. This chapter asks, "In view of the elements which make for growing churches, what response to the Gospel is possible in Mexico today and tomorrow?"

The responsiveness of Mexico has changed enormously in the last twenty years. As the Social Revolution, with its wonderful highways, factories, capital city, and educational system, has created a new land, so the elements we have recounted have ushered in new possibilities of Evangelical increase.

True, the old lingers on. It would be easy to fill pages with accounts of current opposition to Evangelical Churches. Burnings, stonings, priest-led processions, running Evangelicals out of town for singing hymns with a man interested in the Gospel, smashing every pane of glass in a church, mocking a communion service, and threatening the life of new converts — these are common occurrences. When the Union Evangelical Church was built in the best section of Mexico City in 1958, a stone was thrown through the head of Christ in the stained glass window. In some parts of Mexico, Evangelical witness is still hazardous. Yet these are the activities typical of a bygone age. They will diminish, not increase.

In an Evangelical church in the high, dry heart of Roman Catholic Mexico, where Evangelicals have not multiplied in either capital cities or countryside, a convert told us he had first heard the Gospel in the church. We expressed surprise that he should have gone to an Evangelical church — which is prohibited by Roman Catholic priests. He replied, "I did not know of the prohibition, and if I had, I would have gone with even greater gusto." He is not the only Roman Catholic of this independence. He is symptomatic of the new day.

Professor Juan Dias of the Union Theological Seminary in Mexico City says, "Beyond question, we live in a new day of receptiveness. We must change our expectations and our methods to fit it." Christian mission in a moderating religious climate must fashion its strategy to tomorrow, not to yesterday. When growth of the Church was genuinely impossible — converts were driven from their jobs, threatened, or killed, halls could not be rented for evangelistic services, and plots for churches were impossible to buy — gradualistic approaches were good sense. Missions had to "do something else now in the hope of people becoming disciples of Christ later on." But now the climate has changed. In the same towns other denominations are planting churches. *Hacendados* who can drive a convert from his ancestral *rancho* are increasingly rare. Open-air preaching of the Gospel is done and plots are purchased for Evangelical church buildings. Today a gradualistic approach is not good sense.

Church policy today should be framed in the light of this new and increasing responsiveness caused by these elements. When a Church or Board of Missions has ten or a hundred men to assign or ten thousand or a hundred thousand *pesos* or dollars to spend, it should commit them not in patterns which fit 1927 but those which fit 1970. Laborers should not be used to weed or sow when bending heads of yellow wheat nod from certain sections of the field. Indirect evangelism is not called for when direct evangelism yields fruit.

The elements making for church growth have meaning for the entire program and strategy of both Church and Mission.

7 An Experiment by a Static Church

by John Huegel

The Christian Church (Disciples of Christ) is one of the Branches[1] of the Church of Christ in Mexico which has been static. While some other denominations have been getting substantial church growth, the Christian Church has been, until very recently, at a virtual standstill. An experiment in church growth by this old-line denomination attracts our attention in this chapter.

The Christian Church entered Mexico in 1895 and set to work in the northern states of Coahuila and Nuevo Leon. By 1908 there were 900 members in nine churches. Due to the revolution, membership had dropped to 485 by 1915. In 1917 the Foreign Christian Missionary Society of the Christian Church, abiding by the comity agreements of the Cincinnati Plan, surrendered its churches in the north and moved into the state of Aguascalientes, San Luis Potosi, and Zacatecas, to take over work in the area which had been under the direction of the Methodists and Presbyterians. Because the National (Mexican) Presbyterian Church had never approved of the plan, its three churches in the state capitals refused to change affiliation. Some of the rural churches also remained Presbyterian. Only five of the small town congregations became a part of the Christian Church.

The move to this new territory caused the membership of the Christian Church to drop to 350 in 1924. With certain

1 Each Branch of the Church of Christ has its own church growth problem. This chapter tells how one Branch sought to extend the grace of God to more and more people. We believe the story will be helpful to sister communions.

ups and downs, it finally reached about 800 members in 1959. When the Executive Chairman of the Division of World Mission of the United Christian Missionary Society visited the field in May, 1956, and pointed out the static nature of the Church, questions arose in the minds of some missionaries. A series of study institutes was held during 1959 to determine the factors which had arrested church growth and the remedial measures which might be taken. National workers and missionaries, who for years had been satisfied with the static situation, began to review the problem and investigate it. *The Bridges of God* by Donald McGavran, *The Indigenous Church* by Melvin Hodges, and *Missionary Methods: St. Paul's or Ours* by Ronald Allen were widely read and discussed. All of this set the stage for the developments of 1960.

The situation of the Christian Church in January of 1960 was as follows. The 800 members were divided almost equally in two homogeneous units, half in two city churches with predominantly middle-class memberships, and the rest in thirteen widely scattered rural churches and six churchlets. Four different Mexicos were represented in this picture: the "Conservative Cities" of Aguascalientes and San Luis Potosi, seven "Tight Little Towns," ten "Revolutionary Ranchos and Ejidos," and two "Roman Ranchos." At this time there were four ordained pastors, seven paid lay workers, and seventeen missionaries. The mission supported the following institutions: a fully accredited elementary school, a kindergarten, and a social center and library in San Luis Potosi; a fully organized community center and a hospital in Aguascalientes; a girls' hostel and a farm and training school in Pabellon; and one clinic in the Valley of Jerez. The mission also contributed funds and a faculty member to the Union Theological Seminary in Mexico City.

Dr. R. Kenneth Strachan, the General Director of the Latin America Mission, was the speaker for the Annual Assembly in February of 1960. He had just initiated the Evangelism in Depth program in Nicaragua, and presented the

background and basic outline of this movement.[2]   The thesis
on which Evangelism in Depth is based is that the relative
growth of a Church is in direct proportion to the number
of members actively engaged in the continuous propagation
of its message.   The Holy Spirit used Dr. Strachan's messages
as the spark to light the wood which had been gathered during the institutes of 1959.   In a dramatic moment during the
last session of the Assembly, the delegates approved the rough
draft of what was to become the "Plan Revolucionario de
Evangelizacion" (Revolutionary Plan of Evangelization)
commonly known as P.R.E.   During a planning conference
in April, delegates from all of the churches of the field, missionaries, and national workers drew up the plans which set
the program in operation on June 5, 1960.

On that date the directors started out to visit each church
in the field and present in detail the plans which had been
made.   Armed with maps, blackboards, and special flip charts,
they attempted to awaken each church to its God-given task
of evangelism.   Immediately following this first series of
visits, a field-wide prayer campaign was launched.   Prayer
cards were distributed in the churches, and a prayer letter
was sent to more than 2,000 friends in the United States and
other parts of the world.   Different editions of this prayer
letter were sent until the end of the program in 1962.   The
various committees, composed of nationals and missionaries,
were formed and began to function in the fall of 1960.   The
categories included: prayer, finances, equipment, literature,
music, training, visitation, statistics, publicity, and exploration.

The year of 1961 was dedicated to the training and prep-
aration of each member and each church.   A seminary student
gave the first six months of the year to exploration and study
of the field.   He had members of twelve different churches
give him names of relatives or intimate friends in neighboring villages; these would later receive an evangelistic visit.
He thus located 170 villages where there was at least one way

2 R. Kenneth Strachan, *Evangelism in Depth* (Moody Press, 1961).

for the Gospel to enter. He also identified three totally new areas where responsive "Revolutionary Ranchos" were located.

The directors devoted their time during the whole year to holding thirty-seven institutes in the local churches. In each church, one week was dedicated to the study of a simplified version of the Epistle to the Romans, illustrated with chalk drawings, and the second week to practical training in communicating the Gospel to friends and relatives. A total of 716 persons was enrolled.

The pastors and workers preached revival services in eighteen different churches, during which there were thirty-five confessions of faith This interchange of pastors on a field-wide basis served as practical training for future evangelistic campaigns.

In view of the fact that other denominations worked together with the Christian Church in the cities of Aguascalientes and San Luis Potosi, the efforts in those two cities were interdenominational. Local committees were formed in October of 1961 to divide each city into districts for the visitation campaign and to make plans for the city-wide preaching missions which were scheduled for the summer of 1962.

Early in 1962 most pastors and some missionaries went to the World Vision Retreat for Pastors in Guatemala City. The inspiration received from this gathering aroused enthusiasm for the evangelistic endeavors of the year. A final training period of eight weeks in February, March, and April, drew Christians from all over the field into more active participation. Mr. Sam Clark of the mission board, Navigators, Inc., taught the series of eight classes, one each week, in four different centrally located churches. Each neighboring church sent a lay delegate to the central class, and the layman returned to his local church to teach what he had learned. Fifteen local institutes, each with its lay teacher, were held. The total enrollment for the local and central institutes was 245. Testimonies of great sacrifice and commitment came out of this eight-week period. One layman traveled sixty miles each week on a bicycle over rough terrain to attend the central classes. Another sacrificed a total of sixteen working days, traveled 650 miles by bus, and paid twenty dollars during the eight-week period to take the classes.

In March a visitation campaign was launched. Each city church was to visit from house to house and cover as many blocks of its allotted district as possible. Members of rural churches were to visit relatives and intimate friends in neighboring villages. Due to lack of continued supervision, this phase of the program did not bear the expected fruit, especially in the cities.

A final institute in Pabellon drew laymen from all the rural churches for final instructions for the rural preaching missions which were to follow. Eleven students from the Union Theological Seminary in Mexico City (five Disciples, five Methodists, and one Congregationalist), two workers, and one layman were grouped into four teams and sent out for six weeks in April and May to hold preaching missions of one week's duration in eighteen villages and towns. In some cases, a second team followed the first to hold another week of services. Sometimes a team spent one week visiting new villages. Each team received valuable help from laymen, ordained pastors, and workers. Many open-air services were held. An aggregate total of 7,688 people attended the services, 94 confessions of faith and 231 reconsecrations were registered, and ten new villages were visited. For some churches, these had been the first evangelistic campaigns in years. A follow-up program, including literature and Bible study courses, was then brought by Miss Florine Cantrell to each church where confessions of faith had been made.

After the rural campaigns had been finished, attention was given to the two cities of Aguascalientes and San Luis Potosi, where the local committees had been at work for several months. In these two "Conservative Cities" the Evangelicals demonstrated a marked fear complex, especially in San Luis Potosi. There even the pastors had an almost paralyzing fear of what might happen in open-air evangelistic meetings. Excuses and delays were presented at each meet-

ing of the committee, but as the dates drew near, the Holy
Spirit filled all in both cities with new courage and determi-
nation.

Publicity for the campaigns began to appear: advertise-
ments in the newspapers, fliers given out on the streets, posters
on the corners, and spot announcements on the radio.

In each city the services were held in a church during
the first week and in a public place during the second week.
In Aguascalientes a parking lot near the center of town was
rented, and chairs, platform, sound equipment, and lights
were provided. Each evening for a week the Gospel was
proclaimed to a small, but valiant, group of listeners and to
the passers-by. In San Luis Potosi the auditorium of one of
the labor unions was rented and adorned with Bible texts
and red and blue ribbon. The average evening attendance
was 240 persons, but the closing Sunday service drew 485 persons from all walks of life, including the president of the
local chapter of the Communist Party! They heard a thirty-
five voice choir and a visiting soloist sing the praises of God
and a young university student preach the saving message
of Christ.

Although only forty-five persons confessed Christ during
the campaigns in the two cities, a real impact was made on
each city. The Evangelicals were fortified in the faith and
liberated from their blinding fear. They saw that they could
gather in public to proclaim their message with no persecution and with the protection of their government.

No judgment can be made yet as to whether this experiment will result in real church growth. However, some significant steps in that direction have been taken. First of all,
between January 1 and June 30, 1962, in the campaigns and
local church efforts, over 240 registered decisions for Christ
were made. This not only indicates an increased interest in
evangelism on the part of the Church, but it shows that people
in central Mexico do respond to the call of Christ. It is not
yet known how many of these have been baptized and are
actively engaged in the life of local churches. This experi-

ment has shown the leaders of the Church that aggressive evangelism does bear fruit and it has created in their minds a desire for church growth. This experiment was the first church-wide effort which united all missionaries and nationals in one program designed to produce church growth.

As a result of this two-year campaign, two churchlets grew to full church size (ten or more full members) and two abandoned churches regained life and members. The Gospel was preached regularly to people in seven new communities and to fourteen intermittently, in which communities there is every reason to believe that churchlets and churches may develop. In almost every church in the field one hears of new villages where people have requested that someone come with the Gospel or villages where there are natural bridges of relationship or friendship. All this denotes a change in the expectations and climate.

Never before in the sixty-seven-year history of the Christian Church in Mexico have as many church members been actively engaged in some form of proclamation of the faith. Three churches now have groups of laymen who visit a total of twelve or more neighboring villages to hold services and make personal calls. Laymen have studied the Bible, taught classes, preached, traveled, visited, and proclaimed the Gospel as never before; and if they can be further trained in churchmanship and led to witness in the responsive areas which have been found, this will unquestionably lead to church growth.

The results of the P.R.E. (Plan Revolucionario de Evangelization) have caused Disciples leaders to think seriously about the future and begin to prepare a strategy for a growing Church. Plans have been appproved for the division of the field into districts with an ordained pastor as supervisor of each district. An unsalaried lay ministry will be trained to meet the needs of each local rural congregation. The first training session for the ordained pastor-supervisors was held in August of 1962, and the month-long training session for the unsalaried lay leaders was held in February of 1963.

Institutes will be held in each church, during which the lay elders and the members will receive training for carrying on the work of the local church. A new organization will give the laymen responsibility and a voice in the decisions of an association of churches; it is hoped that a genuinely Mexican church structure will thus be erected.

In spite of the apparent success of the Christian Church experiment, some formidable roadblocks appear before it on the road to real church growth. These, by the help of God, must be skillfully overcome:

(1) Have the effects of decades of non-growth been overcome by two years of evangelistic activity? Do the pastors and missionaries still see their roles in the light of a static Church? What is their posture before this new day of opportunity in responsive Mexico? Are expectations at heart still low? If this is the case, then the intervention of God is needed to blast all negativism and faithless expectations out of their minds.

(2) Side by side with the P.R.E. there has been an investment of more than $100,000 (U.S. currency) in capital projects for institutions connected with the Christian Church in Mexico. This outlay of funds necessitates increased personnel and attention. The very grave danger exists of falling back into the institutional pattern of past years. The fundamental question the Christian Church in central Mexico must answer is this: "Do we want church growth, and are we willing to pay the price for it?"

(3) Have the ordained pastors caught the vision of their new role as district supervisors? Are they willing to undertake the hard footwork and pay the price the task entails? If they fail to see that their primary responsibility is now to a circuit and not to a local church, to a group of eager lay elders (the unpaid ministers of local congregations) and not to the Christians who make up these congregations, then the basic plan being developed can hardly succeed.

(4) Can responsive areas be located and visited periodi-

cally by laymen and pastors, so that churchlets and churches may be developed? Much exploration is needed.

(5) Many members of rural churches are in a precarious economic condition because of recent droughts and crop failures. How will this condition affect the amount of time which each lay elder can give to his congregation?

(6) Most small Evangelical congregations in central Mexico tend to become sealed off[3] from the community. What causes this, and how can it be avoided? The connections of members of the Christian churches in Mexico with the general community are amazingly poor, despite forty years in the central part of the country.

A series of suggestions as to what might be done to help the Christian Church overcome the roadblocks and assure church growth seems in order:

(1) Several missionary couples with the church growth point of view are desperately needed. They should be placed in rural areas to work side by side with national pastors. This would help convince the national Church that the mission is truly interested in church growth. At the present time not one missionary is working with a national pastor in a village. Concentration of missionaries in the cities, chiefly at the institutions, is not the right policy for the future.

(2) By March of 1963 there were eight Disciples students preparing for the ministry in the Union Theological Seminary in Mexico City. It is imperative that they receive a point of view which emphasizes church growth. The program of the seminary at the present time seems to be training men who will serve already established churches rather than teaching men how to establish new ones. Perhaps some present faculty member could be trained in church growth, and then he could give his time to teaching and communicating this. The Congregational and Methodist churches who also use the Seminary would greatly profit by this emphasis. The

3 Becoming "sealed off" versus maintaining good connections is discussed in Chapter 10.

same person might teach at four other seminaries in Mexico City: Baptist, Lutheran, Presbyterian, and Episcopal.

(3) Mexico City is most responsive. It must receive special attention by the Christian Church. Trained personnel should dedicate full time to planting new churches in this teeming metropolis.

(4) Funds must be made available for new church lots and buildings. Churches should not be pauperized, but helped in a sound, constructive way. One church, in La Reforma, S.L.P., has been building a stone structure for over four years, but because of drought and bad economic conditions, the church is not yet finished. This is disheartening.

(5) An attempt must be made to hive the city churches in Aguascalientes and San Luis Potosi. Responsive sections of each city, new colonies, government housing projects, or industrial sections could be selected for the location of new churches.

(6) A special effort should be made to locate more "Revolutionary Ranchos and Ejidos" where responsiveness is still high. Attention and personnel must then be dedicated to them.

(7) Special literature for conditions which the Church is facing should be printed or made available to pastors and laymen. Tracts and a layman's manual are especially needed.

(8) A new day of freedom and non-intervention on the part of the government is at hand. Not only the Church but also church-related institutions must make the most of this and develop an aggresive evangelistic witness. In the past, some of the outstanding members of the church in Aguascalientes have come from the English classes taught in the community center. More people can be brought into the Church through the institutions. Everyone knows these institutions are Evangelical. The Gospel should be clearly sounded forth from them.

(9) Mexico has seven million radios, according to a recent study. Almost every home in the cities has a radio, and many rural families have a radio as their one luxury. Central

Mexico needs an Evangelical radio station. The possibility of establishing one in Zacatecas or San Luis Potosi should be seriously studied.

8 A Mestizo People Movement

Whenever a homogeneous population, from whatever cause, finds a Christward surge going through it, such that groups of interrelated individuals become Christian, we say, "A people movement to Christ is going on." Chains of individuals and small groups, each well instructed, come to faith. In any one year the number of persons converted may be only a few hundred, but over twenty years a Church of many thousands results. People movements have brought in more than two-thirds of the membership of the younger Churches around the world. To find them in Mexico is not surprising. Such a people movement to Christ has surged across the Mestizo population of the state of Tabasco.

The conditions necessary for large people movements exist neither in Mexican cities nor in the typical *ranchos* and *pueblos* of most of the land. But the young people of each *rancho,* in the great . majority of cases, marry young women of the same *rancho.* The interrelated families form a small web of kinship, sociologically similar to the large web in Tabasco. Churches all over Mexico can, therefore, study with profit how the Presbyterian Church has grown in Tabasco. This case of church growth is replete with lessons.

Presbyterian growth in Tabasco can be divided into three periods: 1884-1924, 1925-1935, and 1936-1962.

Period One, 1884-1924.

In 1884 Rev. Eligio Granados, a Mexican from near Mexico City, was ordained and sent to Tabasco. He worked there until his death in 1923. Small Presbyterian churches were gradually established in the towns of Comalcalco, Paraiso, Cardenas, Villahermosa, and smaller ones in four others. American missionaries visited there from Vera Cruz or resided there briefly — the last one from 1924 to 1927. Church growth, however, was due to the work of the Mexican ministers, Granados and Diaz, and to lay witness. The institutional approach, common in other parts of Mexico, was noticeably absent — though Mr. Granados in 1922 yearned for "a school, a church and a dispensary" in each of the larger towns!

Church growth in Period One was ordinary. In 1922 Mr. Granados wrote a careful memoir of the work in which the only hint of membership is where he says of the congregation in Villahermosa (the capital and his own residence for many years) that there were 276 names on the roll, "of whom most are now in the Kingdom of God." This means that in 1922 there was a living membership of perhaps one hundred in Villahermosa and vicinity. Comalcalco was said to be "a somewhat larger work," and there were churches in Paraiso, Cardenas, and four other towns. Each town congregation had some country members. Comalcalco and Paraiso in 1926 had church buildings, but Evangelicals in Villahermosa and other towns met in homes or rented buildings. If we estimate membership at Comalcalco at 150 and the others at 100 members each, we get a total membership of the Presbyterian Church in 1922 of less than 1,000, concentrated in the towns.

The Roman Catholic Church had neglected hot, swampy Tabasco and had placed few priests there. The upper classes lived in towns near the priests; but the peasants seldom saw one. Nevertheless, the peasants had their infants baptized in the church. The isolation of the country folk had a great bearing on later church growth, but not much before 1930. Till 1930 the main body of Evangelicals was in the towns.

Period Two, 1925-1935.

Between 1925 and 1930 the Church grew little, if any. The days were unsettled. Mr. Granados had died. A missionary followed Mr. Granados, but withdrew in 1927. Agrarian revolt was shaking Mexico. Yucatecan Ezequiel Lango, on mission salary, came to Tabasco in 1926 and stayed until 1930. He feels that persecution was more vigorous then than in 1930-35.[1]

In 1930 Governor Garrido Canabal came to Tabasco and resolved to wipe out Christianity entirely. He closed all churches and sent priests and ministers out of the state. He ordered saints buried and Bibles burned. His regime lasted until 1935. Dr. John Mackay is said to have visited Tabasco in 1935 and reported that "there is nothing left here of the Church" — so thoroughly had it been driven underground.

Five years of persecution by the state proved a turning point in church growth. Persecution is not always good for a Church, but this time it was. Persecution grievously afflicted the Roman Catholics. Since they were accustomed to being the State Church and doing what Authority commanded, they did not know how to meet official prohibition. Evangelicals had been accustomed to persecution by the Church of Rome and did not require official approval to flourish. Roman Catholics, ordered to bury their saints, did so. Evangelicals, ordered to burn their Bibles, continued to read them in secret and to invite others to hear the prohibited Word of God. Masses ceased to be celebrated, but Evangelical worship around the Bible flourished. The towns were too dangerous, so services were held in rural homes along the rivers or back in the swamps.

The son-in-law of Rev. Eligio Granados, Sr. Quaquin Vera, now the treasurer of the Presbytery, felt that about a third of the Evangelicals left Tabasco during 1930-35, a tenth reverted to the world, and nevertheless, after the persecution, there were twice as many Christians as before. Other informants thought that numbers dropped off during the persecution and growth did not start until after 1935. Records, of course, were not kept.

Since those leaving Tabasco would not have been peas-

[1] From an interview with him in August, 1962, in Mexico City.

ants who owned land and who were relatively secure in their isolated holdings, but rather town dwellers, and since the meetings were held in the country and not in the towns, what Governor Canabal probably achieved was to drive the Evangelical Church, which already had some rural members, out into the country where it spread quietly. Town Christians were weakened and country Christians strengthened. Various stories bear out this assumption. "We were meeting in a *rancho* at night and heard the soldiers coming. We fell on our faces in prayer, and they took a fork in the road and passed fifty meters from our house." "Christians met in jungle places. The grapevine told them when and where." "We had an Evangelical horse which helped us greatly. When it heard anyone coming, it would turn into the bushes and stand quietly till the person went by. Thus our leaders reached their meetings unobserved."

In 1934 or 1935 Ezequiel Lango and Calixto Lugo from Yucatan made "a rapid journey through Tabasco, strengthening and confirming the brethren." They planned to stay two jumps ahead of the police.

Four new churches were established during the persecution. It is important to note that this "Mestizo People Movement" was led very largely by laymen. Barely literate peasant Christians taught, witnessed, and spread the faith. Some mission evangelists (such as Ezequiel Lango) of the twenties left the state in 1930. Others merged into the unpaid lay leadership.

Period Three, 1936-1962.

In 1936, when regulations against religion were relaxed, the Presbyterian Church, purged and invigorated by the years underground, burst into exceptional growth. This growth continued unabated through 1947. A few instances can be mentioned.

In 1938 Calixto Lugo again visited Tabasco, preached to a total of 13,000, baptized 458, and received 363 into membership.

In 1943 a visitor wrote, "Work here far surpasses all I have been told. The persecutions of former years are bearing fruit now in the eagerness with which the Gospel is heard."

In 1943 also, when the James McKaughans came to Tabasco, "a group of laymen from 15 to 20 rural congregations came into Comalcalco every Thursday afternoon to prepare, under guidance, the service they were to conduct in their hamlets on Sunday. They went back out Thursday evening. Country people preaching to country people was the system. All were volunteers and unpaid."

In that great decade, growth was neither automatic nor easy. A typical church history follows. The Sinai church began with a group of believers in 1937. When the house they were meeting in was burned by Roman Catholics, they built a pole-and-thatch church. It was completed on Christmas Day, 1938 — and burned by the Roman Catholics the same day. The very next day the Evangelicals met to put up another church. It was completed in a week. Later a brick church was built, and recently a 40-by-110-foot sanctuary, to cost 150,000 *pesos* given by the people themselves, has been begun and will be completed in five years.

About 1947 a visitor wrote: "Everywhere little new churches are being formed. Bamboo walls, thatch roofs, and mud floors are all that meets the eye. Every Sunday and often on week days, congregations gather by boat or horse. Enthusiastic men and women recently won by the Gospel meet to worship. The number reached and won depends only on the number of workers willing to give up everything for Christ and spend themselves in this tropical, swampy, malaria-infested region."

As in all people movements, growth followed the web of relationship. Chains of families (most of them whole families) came into the old churches or established new ones.

Like all people movements among rural people in roadless country, the worshiping groups with their thatch-roofed chapels, led entirely by laymen, were difficult to fit into a neat, tidy system. With no ministers at all during 1930-35, and only six by 1948, accurate records were unknown. Many believers — sincere, convinced Evangelicals — could not be baptized and put on the rolls because ministers were not present. So worshiping groups grew up with unbaptized and baptized believers all functioning as "the church."

Churches consisting of a core of baptized, on-the-roll Christians and a fringe of unbaptized believers are common in Mexico. In Tabasco, however, this fringe was more intimately related to the core, since it enjoyed some of the responsibilities of church membership. Two questions arise. (a) Ought membership in Tabasco to be estimated as consisting of all believers who are integral parts of the Evangelical community and intermarry with it and are confessedly Evangelicals? Or only of full, regular, baptized members? If the latter, then Tabasco has probably only six or seven thousand members. If the former, then it has probably twelve to fourteen thousand.   (b) How much was growth of the Evangelicals in Tabasco aided by the fact that improperly married believers could become members of the church in a pragmatic sense (attend, give, build the church, intermarry, call themselves Evangelicals) without the constant, galling disapproval of official church leaders and without thinking of themselves as "irregular," "sinful," or "not saved"?

Did freedom (during 1930-40) from too close ministerial and missionary control help growth? All over Mexico, would it be better to leave discipline and "excluding from community" to the local churches — as Anglican Roland Allen insists was the New Testament practice? A careful study of this question in Tabasco by a convinced Pauline man who is also a competent social scientist would be illuminating.

In 1947 or 1948 a special effort was made to secure a total membership figure. Don Hermilio Granados, son of the pioneer minister, told us it proved to be 10,000 and was overwhelmingly rural.

In 1948 missionaries began a system of lay-leadership training and evangelistic campaigning. They took a preaching and training team to the country churches. An airplane and pilot from the Missionary Aviation Fellowship helped transportation in roadless, swampy country. Seventy congregations built air strips. By 1956, 125 three-day institutes a year were being held, about 25 to 30 a month. The threefold purpose was to strengthen believers by powerful preaching, to prepare workers for service in churches, and to evangelize the unsaved. New worshiping groups were established in considerable numbers. In recent years (1959-62) the number of institutes has been cut down to about 40 a year. The increase in the number of Bible School trained workers has changed the nature of the institute program to some extent. Institutes are now more regional in nature and have a more specific purpose. They train in stewardship, personal evangelism, Sunday school teaching and the like.

During the last few years the Church has been growing in new communities. Tabasco has much jungle land. As this is cleared and drained and roads are built, new communities spring up. In these, Evangelicals are quite successful in planting churches. Mr. McKaughan, veteran missionary, says there is also much opportunity in older places.

A few congregations comprise almost everyone in the locality, but the common pattern is Evangelicals scattered throughout the countryside among "Roman Catholic" neighbors. There is, therefore, a very large "worldly reservoir" from which the Church can grow enormously. Out of a total population of 400,000, only a tenth is now counted in the Evangelical community. Active full members may not be more than 7,000. Membership is greatest where there is the largest population.

Christians in rural areas are numerous enough so that whole families (husband and wife both Evangelicals) are the rule and Evangelical young people marry Evangelicals. There is some evidence that half families (only one partner an active, full member and the other a worldly Evangelical) are common. If this is generally true, the Evangelical community includes both an Evangelical Church and an Evangelical world.

Missionaries and national leaders agree that great opportunity for growth continues.

In Comalcalco, at the Dorcas Bible School, are 13 young women. In Villahermosa Bible School are 12 young men in training as lay leaders. This latter number ought at once to be increased to at least fifty. A church of 25,000 full members by 1975 should come about, and it will require many more and better trained laymen than a twelve-student Bible school and three-day institutes can create. Sizeable amounts of "mission money" can be used in stipends for Bible-school students to the great benefit of the Church.

The Presbytery now (1962) includes 15 ministers, about 20 paid and partly paid workers, a multitude of unpaid lay leaders, 24 churches and about 200 congregations and preaching points. The 200 should be understood as "large and small worshiping groups of baptized and unbaptized believers." Most congregations, and some preaching points, have their own church buildings — pole and thatch, or brick and galvanized iron sheets. The 24 central churches are, of course, well-housed.

Firm membership figures for today could not be obtained. Some responsible leaders said 7,000, some 10,000, and some 12,000. Ten thousand full members in 1947 was the firmest figure we obtained, and it was supported by several sources. Mr. Denman, Presbyterian missionary in Tabasco, pointed out that it was based on a real census. The best informed nationals we interviewed estimated that at present there are 12,000 full members, 25,000 believers, and a total community of 50,000 to 70,000. Missionaries were inclined to cut the full active membership down to 7,000 or even 5,000.

It would seem highly desirable for the Presbyterian Church to spend a few thousand dollars for an accurate, locally verified, membership count. How can a battle be fought when no one knows where the troops are? How can the church plan its strategy when the figures seem to prove a disastrous slowdown, but everyone thinks the churches are growing greatly? How can the mission assist the Church intelligently without knowing the rates and places of increase?

The following graph, *an approximation,* is attempted because a graph of growth helps us visualize what has really happened. This is its only excuse. Some such graph as this will account for the Tabasco story recounted by the leaders of the presbytery. One point at which the recounted facts do not fit the story is the present membership. If 10,000 in 1947 is a correct figure, and the growth of the last 15 years has been as great as everyone says it has been, then the membership today will not be 12,000 but 15,000 or even 20,000. Growing churches often double in ten years. The church has had some conversion growth and, with the population explosion, should have had great biological growth. Also, fifteen to twenty thousand seems likely, unless the 10,000 of 1947 is a greatly exaggerated figure. However, we must not speculate. We take the facts given from several different sources. They affirm the membership in 1948 was 10,000 and today is 12,000.

If these figures are correct,[2] then the church in Tabasco has practically ceased growing. An increase of 2,000 full members in 14 years (1948-1962) is not even good biological growth. The matter is of such great importance that we set forth the facts given us hoping that (a) if they are correct, Church and mission will take speedy steps to recapture church growth; and (b) if they are incorrect, the truth will be made available so that it can guide policy decisions.

Tabasco church growth cannot be reproduced in other parts of Mexico. Governor Canabal's attempt to stamp out Christianity will not be duplicated. Nevertheless, this vigor-

2 One well-informed missionary, on seeing this graph, preferred the picture presented by the dotted line. Rev. Fred G.Tinley writes, "The 10,000 of 1948 must represent the full Evangelical community, or possibly the baptized members including children. I judge the present Evangelical community at about 20,000 to 25,000. There is a lack of system in preparing believers for baptism and receiving new converts and young people into full membership. There is at least a sixty percent loss of young people of the church due to lack of adequate care of this second generation."

TABASCO CHURCH GROWTH
AN APPROXIMATION

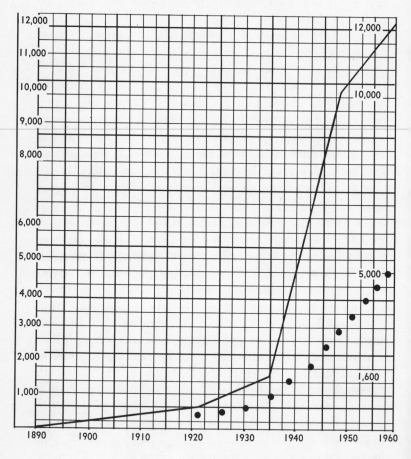

ous Church teaches us many lessons. Some of these are as follows.

(1) The little town churches of the twenties in Tabasco, because of being driven out by the persecution, found *responsive neglected people* who own their own land and were therefore free to follow their consciences. Evangelical Churches in other states need not wait till persecution drives them to the responsive. They can seek them out at once.

(2) Tabasco Christians were willing *to pay the price*. The account of the Sinai church is but one of many stories of heroism. A missionary from Chiapas and church leaders from Yucatan toured Tabasco on foot by stealth and *against the law* during 1930-36, baptizing and marrying at night and encouraging a daring and devout (but ignorant) Church. Innumerable laymen performed acts of faith and courage.

(3) The absolute necessity of *intensive and widespread evangelism* by the people is an impressive lesson. Tabasco cannot be explained by the persecution. That was the stage setting. After the persecution was over, in 1936-47, church growth was caused by visitation, persuasion, evangelism, and Bible teaching to people of the world. Hundreds of thousands of miles were walked, rowed, and ridden, by men carrying the Gospel.

(4) The *leadership of the common people* was abundantly validated. Leaders of the Church were (and still are) horny-handed Tabascanians, speaking Spanish with a Tabascanian twang. Tabascanian Christians are so countrified that to date Christian ministers from the privileged middle class churches of the highlands who on rare occasions have visited here have been rather unimpressed with church growth in Tabasco! There were only two ministers in Tabasco before 1930, and only six in 1955 for more than 10,000 active believers. There were no missionaries between 1927 and 1940. All leaders (Sunday school teachers, deacons and elders, leaders of worship services, chairmen of boards and committees) came straight out of rural churches in which,

among the older people, there is still much illiteracy. Such
humble leaders in Presbyterian churches are common in
India and Africa. Old-line Churches in Mexico need to learn
that Christian discipleship is not cultural uplift. The Bible
does not teach that crude illiterate people cannot be saved.
Indeed, the early Church — to the cultured people of Jerusa-
lem — appeared to be led by "ignorant and unlearned men."

(5) Almost all church buildings were pole-and-thatch
structures at first. Many such "temples" exist today. This is a
Church of the common people who build churches they can
afford. The Evangelical Church has exploded among the
masses in Tabasco. (The Tabascanian *classes* have always
been, and still *are,* resistant. Had the Presbyterian Church
concentrated on them it would still be a very small affair.)
A Church of the masses is exceedingly precious. *The masses
are worth winning.* Tomorrow belongs to them. As Tabasco
becomes the bread basket of Mexico, and the huge oil and
gas reserves beneath her are developed, the economic level of
Evangelicals will rise.

(6) These churches — partly as a result of growth and
partly as a cause of growth — *consist of whole families.* A typical congregation might have 30 men, 34 women, 20 big boys
and 22 big girls. This "whole family" character makes for an
enduring, reproducing community.

(7) The mode of evangelism has been *quiet action by
Mexicans on foot.* Foot soldiers may not explain the Bible as
correctly as mechanized troops would do, but they reach the
unsaved more effectively. The Presbyterian Church in Tabasco looks like a Mexican Church — assisted by one missionary family to several thousand active believers. Mexican
proclamation of Christ is effective. It flows quietly to relatives and intimates, with no jeep announcing its arrival and no
Roman-Catholic-directed counteraction possible during the
incubation period.

(8) The *skill of common people in presenting the Gospel and persuading their fellows to accept membership in the*

Evangelical Church is one of the lessons of Tabasco. The common people work out effective presentations — sometimes crude — of which the ministry, Mexican and American, would not dream. A Tabascanian told me, "When prohibition came (1930), the Roman Catholics buried their saints. When they dug them up in 1936, they had all rotted. We Evangelicals used to say, 'Have you heard about the saints they dug up at San Pedro?' Then our relatives and friends would laugh. They would see how powerless the plaster saints really are and how God has appointed only one Priest, Jesus Christ." Common people know best what will strike home to their intimates and convince them.

(9) The *joy of simple biblical worship,* with the Bible open and understandable, was part of the secret of growth. So was *changed life.* "Before I became a Christian I never had enough money to clothe my children. I spent what I earned on drink, gambling, and other sins. After I became a Christian, my life improved. I bought more land. I prospered. My relatives see it is good to be an Evangelical." This Christian testimony, common all around the world, has been given to good effect by thousands in Tabasco.

(10) *The great program of lay training,* carried on by the Tabasco missionaries since 1948, has lifted the Church both in quantity and quality. Missionaries have operated on the sound basis that lay leadership is the most precious asset any Church possesses. Their efforts to develop lay leaders in local churches and remote hamlets have been invaluable.

Some competent student of comparative church growth should tell the Tabasco story after combing the archives in New York and spending three months in Tabasco itself. He would interview present leaders, old members, new converts, the first churches, and the last churches. He would analyze dozens of church rolls, name by name, and make family analyses of the membership and community. Until that scientific account is made and published, however, this story of a notable case of church growth in Mexico, picked up on a brief visit, will have to suffice.

*   *   *   *   *

What of the future for the Presbyterian Church in Tabasco? Its community is now only a tenth of the population. Can it, in the next ten years, become a half — 200,000? Or a fifth — 80,000? The answer to these questions depends on the experience, faith, and courage of Presbyterian leaders in Tabasco, Mexico City, and New York. People movements of this size are unknown in Mexico. There is some danger that Presbyterians, comparing Tabasco growth with the tiny growth of highly assisted churches in some parts of Mexico, will feel their chief duty to curb the "run-away" growth and achieve "quality" in Christian living. That quality is highly desirable none will debate; but that growth must be neglected or curbed to achieve it is one of the commonest and most pernicious of mission misjudgments. It afflicts younger Churches and their assisting missions in many lands.

The Tabasco Presbyterian Church is not a large Church. Churches of fifty thousand or a hundred thousand communicants have arisen in many lands. Many Christ-ward movements in large populations consider their first twelve thousand communicants a mere beginning. It would be a pity if the generally poor expectations in regard to church growth in Mexico — especially among the old-line denominations — should impose too low a ceiling on Presbyterians in Tabasco. Or if "Fatigue" (See *How Churches Grow,* Chapter 21) of the small staff in Tabasco operated to the same end.

The Church in Tabasco and its assisting mission face a common condition. They have had a striking early increase. What should they do now "after the first flush of success"?[3]

All around the world several easy and naive answers are given. (1) "We have now achieved our growth. The next stage is consolidation." (2) Missionaries say, "The matter is

[3] Donald McGavran, "After the First Flush of Success," *International Review of Missions* (July, 1959).

not in our hands. All we can do is to limit aid severely. We must throw the younger Church on its own and leave the rest to God." (3) Nationals declare, "What we need now is more money from the missionary society." (4) "We should not be concerned about numbers or organizations. Our sole concern should be for the spiritual life of the existing Church and the education of its members." (5) "What we do, we do well. The historic purpose of our Church is to produce solid, educated Christians. We are not at all impressed with mere numbers of Christians or churches."

These answers — anywhere in the world — miss the mark. They fail to see hundreds of thousands of highly winnable men and women who (if any of the above glib answers is followed) will live without Christ and die in their sins.

Were these answers to be given in Tabasco, they would cause an end to growth. After a glorious beginning in which laymen, ministers, and missionaries brought multitudes to a redemptive relationship to Jesus Christ our Lord, the Presbyterian Church would now become content merely to perfect the existing Christians. At the very time when, with the momentum of a small people movement behind it, this Church could liberate tens of thousands, these answers would emasculate the Church and let those thousands live on in the slavery of sin.

The leadership in Tabasco gives none of these answers. It is not content to stop. It is afraid that Presbyterian leaders outside Tabasco, instead of pushing the Church in Tabasco, are going to drain it of leadership to encourage development in other parts of Mexico and Latin America. It fears the board will limit aid at the very place where *aid properly used* would enable continued vigorous discipling of Tabascanian multitudes.

At present, world mission is assisting the Church in Tabasco at the rate of one missionary to 4000 members of the Evangelical community scattered across difficult terrain. Is this effective aid? Merely to send twenty additional missionaries would not guarantee results — they might be the kind of missionaries whose ideas, convictions, and training would immediately stop all church growth. On the other hand, no principle of church growth is known to the effect that severely limiting missionary aid causes churches to multiply.

"Aid properly used" is a crucial phrase. Most younger Churches need aid in training leaders. Training takes place at three levels: (1) unpaid local church leaders, (2) paid pastors and pastoral workers of small churches, and (3) pastors of big city churches, district superintendents, and national and international leaders. All three should be trained in suitable proportions. Tabasco needs many more of each kind to prepare for a Church of 25,000 communicants in 1975. The present number of churches (24) should be trebled by 1975. To provide 100 ministers (a dozen of them men of national and international caliber who know English and Spanish) and to develop stewardship to pay them is a large assignment. To create 2000 finely trained unpaid laymen to shepherd and feed the multitude of small congregations in Tabasco is an essential goal. Aid which provides all these is "aid properly used."

Because the Presbyterian Church in Mexico has several greatly growing presbyteries — Chiapas, Yucatan, and Tabasco — its thinking is not as static as that of many Evangelical Churches in Mexico. Nevertheless, it should consider the following.

Seminaries all across Christendom, as Bishop Lesslie Newbigin has pointed out, have for hundreds of years been engaged in preparing a ministry for the existing Church, not a ministry to multiply churches across the world. American seminaries are still in this frame of mind. This "Shadow of the North" can fall heavily on the Presbyterian seminary in Mexico as it strives to reach "American standards." We must ask: do seminarians sent up from Tabasco (and from the Chol and Tseltal people movements) receive adequate training in how churches grow, how people movements to Christ are best nurtured and extended, how arrest of movement can be prevented and the second and third generation kept from getting sealed off? If the answer to this question is "no," then much aid can be "properly used" in immediately training a first-class man — Mexican or American — to occupy a chair of Church Growth or Church Dynamics in the Presbyterian seminary in Mexico City.

Some Tabascanian Presbyterians believe a seminary should be set up in Tabasco. They recognize that they must get more Tabascanian ministers who, while in training, should be protected from the academic and foreign influences of the great city. They want them to be effective *in Tabasco*. While their intent is excellent, one may doubt whether merely starting a seminary in Tabasco would meet the need. It is all too possible to start a seminary of the common Christendom variety (engaged in preparing a ministry for the existent Church) and not to multiply churches across Tabasco. Since the problem of Tabasco is also the problem of Chiapas and, potentially, the problem of Yucatan — i.e., how to prepare scores of ministers who know the science of church growth and go back to their posts to nurture and multiply existing churches — aid would be more properly used in helping the Mexico City seminary give effective training in church multiplication than in starting new seminaries.

Since this growing Church is being very slightly assisted, at the rate of one missionary to four thousand of the Presbyterian community (community — 25,000; missionaries, counting wives — 6), should the number be increased to one missionary to 1000 of the community? (Many static Churches in Mexico are assisted at the rate of one missionary to 100). If so, 25 missionaries would be required — an increase of 19. Would this be a good policy?

If by "missionaries" we mean missionaries in general, committed to many good ends, specialists in agriculture, education, church history, nursing, and surgery, with the over-all purpose of "helping the poor Tabascanians," then the answer must be "no." Nineteen such missionaries would stop church growth in Tabasco shortly after their arrival.

If by "missionaries" we mean assistants called by middle-class Presbyterian leaders in Tabasco to establish schools and colleges in which Tabascanian youth may be lifted to middle-class affluence — whether churches multiply or not — then, too, the answer must be a firm "no."

But if by "missionaries" we mean men and women called to and trained for the task of discipling the receptive thousands of Tabasco and located by the presbytery in the most fertile areas, the answer must be a ringing "yes."

The training of laymen, ministers, and missionaries on the scale suggested above should accompany training of a seminary teacher and several first-class men — nationals or missionaries — for the following urgent tasks.

(1) Making an accurate census of Presbyterian and other Evangelical membership in Tabasco. This is no simple task. It involves visiting each of the 220 preaching points, congregations, and churches and going through 220 rolls, name by name. A family chart of each worshipping group is required. It will take a trained man months to do. To be of greatest value, the study should be repeated at two-year intervals, for the growth history of these churches over the next six years will tell us much more than merely identifying their present situation.

(2) Determining where the churches in Tabasco are sealed off, beginning to be sealed off, or rapidly growing.

(3) Determining why each of these processes is taking place. The psychology of growth in the minds of the people and the leaders (the self-images of the congregations and pastors) is of utmost importance here.

(4) Ascertaining what theological, national, economic, and social formulations and convictions lie back of the great growth in 1936-47, and of the slowdown observed in parts of the presbytery today.

(5) Hammering out a program and encouraging a spiritual vitality which will keep every congregation of the Church in Tabasco growing in the highly responsive population which surrounds it.

(6) Assembling now, while many participants are still

alive, a record of the Reformation in Tabasco. Living church history lies before us here, and priceless opportunities to record it are rapidly slipping away. Perhaps some department of church history in a seminary in the United States would invest four thousand dollars and one year to capture this moment of truth in the life of the Church. It would take the Presbyterian Church in Tabasco far less money and time to assemble the stories, but the historical perspective and scholarly discrimination needed might be lacking.

(7) Breaching the barrier in the neighboring state of Vera Cruz. Coastal Tabasco and Vera Cruz are geographically and socially much alike, but the Presbyterian Church has never grown greatly in Vera Cruz. We do not know if the Tabasco fire can be carried across the border, but precedents are not lacking and the possibilities should certainly be explored.

(8) Making a comparative study of — let us say — the Iglesia Apostolica de la Fe with its 10,000 full members among the Spanish-speaking population of Mexico, and the Presbyterian Church of 12,000 full members in Tabasco to see what can be learned of mutual benefit.

A great cloud of witnesses in Mexico surrounds us. These are the heroes of the faith — missionaries, ministers, laymen, laywomen, prophets, and martyrs. They poured out their lives that the Church of Christ in Mexico might be multiplied. They would be the first to demand that, when God has opened the door to growth, we pay particular attention, lest by our existing commitments, our dull eyes, and unbelieving hearts we frustrate the redemptive purposes of God.

9 Indian People Movements

A people is a society which thinks of itself as a separate unit. It marries largely within itself (is endogamous). It often speaks its own language. The majority of its members are commonly of one economic standard and of one culture. The Jews of our Lord's time were " a people." The Navahos are "a people." Each caste in India is "a people." The rural people of Tabasco in 1930 were "a people" in the sense that they were a segment of Mexican population which married largely within itself, felt themselves to be Tabascanians, had about the same economic standards, and spoke one common language. Rural Tabasco was one vast network of interrelated families.

Each Indian segment of the Mexican population, however, is "a people" in a much more radical sense. It has its own language, its own customs, its own leaders — who are different from the Spanish-speaking leaders. It has a high degree of enforced endogamy. It has an intense consciousness of being a separate nation — in the archaic James Fenimore Cooper meaning of "nation," as when he speaks of "the Mohican nation."

Peoples and tribes resist the Christian faith solidly at first. To become Christian is to abandon "our ancestral faith" — be that pagan or Christo-pagan — and to be "a traitor to our nation." But when the Christian faith finds a foothold (after the first 1000 have become Christian in groups) then prospective converts say to themselves, "In becoming Christian, we are not betraying our people; we are leading it on to better things. We are leaving our old-fashioned faith and joining *our own* vanguard of advance." They think of themselves as heroes and trail blazers. Group decision by two and three families (and by twenty and thirty families, too) becomes an ordinary mode of conversion. The faith, once lit in a people, has a chance to grow soundly and rapidly along the all-important web of relationships.

We have seen how the people movement among the Mestizos of rural Tabasco grew and flourished. Let us now see how a people movement developed among the Otomi, Tzeltal, and Chol tribes of Indians. For the account of the Otomis, I am indebted to the Rev. Eugene Lee of Mexico City.

Venancio Hernandez, an Otomi Indian, is a man of exceptional ability. As a boy of ten he was put in charge of a group of *peons* on a *hacienda.* He was converted in the United States as a young man. On his return to Mexico, while working as a foreman in charge of *peons* on a *hacienda,* he resolved to lead his fellow Otomis to Christ. For a year he said nothing to them about Christ, but identified himself with them and worked to improve their living conditions. "I want you to dress better," he said. "You must not squander your money on gambling and drink." The next year he began to speak to them openly about the Saviour. Most of them became Christians.

Venancio was discharged and went to the nearest big town to get work. The *peons,* under pressure to give up their faith, left the *hacienda* and moved, families and all, into town. They had no place to stay. Outside the town was a bare hill of white earth. Venancio obtained permission to settle his relatives and fellow Otomis on it. They built small huts — as refugees anywhere will. Venancio taught them brick laying. He improved a loom and taught them how to weave better cloth. This cloth sold well and improved their income. Today these former refugees live in concrete-block houses and enjoy a much higher standard of living than they formerly did.

Venancio owed his conversion to Pentecostal preaching about the Saviour. He identified his churches with the Independent Evangelical Pentecostals. The Otomis proclaim the faith as they understand the Bible and the Holy Spirit. They hold that conversion is of the whole man. Soul, mouth, hands, feet — all are converted, turned from old sinful ways and given to God's service. Venancio says, "We believe in both the gifts of the Spirit and fruits of the Spirit."

The denomination has spread through the valley and up into the hills. There are 25 churches in the Valle de Mesquital, just north of Mexico City, and 25 in the hills. Communicants number 5000, which means a total community of at least 10,000, created in the last 20 years. While the average church has 100 communicants, there are some of two or three hundred and many of 50 or less. The Otomis are rural people and the size of the congregation is limited by the size of the peasant hamlet.

The worship services are informal. An orchestra — with guitars, cellos and trumpets — plays two or three times in the course of the service. The women's choral group sings several times. Anyone who wants to sing or say something sends a note to the leader and is fitted into the service. Otomi Christians enjoy worship and being together. Meetings sometimes last four or five hours.

Their basic principle in evangelizing new villages is to find out the needs of the village and help the people there. After this has been done, they preach Christ. They tell the people, "The sickness you suffer, we suffered, and Christ has healed us. The burdens you bear, we once bore, and Christ has lifted them off our backs." In one village there was no school. A young convert from an older church went in and started one. All this takes its inspiration from Venancio's initial experience with the *peons* of whom he was the boss. Serve them first; preach Christ after.

Everything they touch they try to redeem. When a village becomes Christian, it puts up a good church building — with suitable help from the older churches. Otomis then build a good road to the church with a bulldozer and a scraper. Through the church, the whole community gets a better road. Communications are redeemed. Otomi Evangelicals have started many basketball teams and built many courts. Recreational life has been redeemed.

20137

Community relations have sweetened. Some Roman Catholics killed an Evangelical — and went to jail for it. They heard the gospel there. When they came out, they became Evangelicals themselves and built a chapel in honor of the man they killed. A fanatical Roman Catholic owned a certain hill and wrote on it, in big white-washed stones, THIS HILL IS ROMAN CATHOLIC. Now converted, he has used these stones to build a church.

Pastors and leaders come up out of the ranks. The Otomis have no Bible school or seminary. They get mature men as pastors — some 25, some 30, and some 65 years of age. Venancio Hernandez himself is about 50 years old. All pastors are literate, all are Otomis, and all are paid on an Otomi scale, that is, about what a normal hard-working man would receive. Pastors dress in ordinary work clothes and do not scorn working their own fields and gardens.

Good works and practical love for the brethren form an important part of the Otomi concept of the Christian's duty. In 1962 the Otomis gathered money to send to a famine-stricken group in the north. Christians in groups, through all kinds of work projects, do many good deeds. Mr. Hernandez believes very much in social service. He has worked out a form of health insurance for his folk.

This is a people movement, i.e., a tribal movement. It has taken place in one tribe, which still speaks the Otomi language. All church services, except that in the central church, are in Otomi, despite the fact that most of the men speak some Spanish. All church members are related and interrelated. All pastors are Otomis. For many years evangelistic efforts were concentrated in Otomi villages and new churches were Otomi churches. All this is typical people movement procedure. But now the movement is spilling over into the Mestizo population. New churches are arising among non-Otomi neighbors. Having grown strong among the Otomis, the faith is now spreading to "the Gentiles."

The Tzeltal and Chol tribes in Chiapas have also turned to Christ. Important leaders became informants for the Wycliffe translators. Through finding out what the Scripture says about sin, salvation, Christ, life, death, and the Church, they became firm believers.

They transmitted the faith to their intimates. Groups of believers began to be baptized, build churches, preach the good news, and add others to the Lord. Unlike the Otomis, social service in advance of the Word has not been their mode of evangelism; but as they have become Christians and built churches, they have been greatly blessed and are surging forward to unimagined prosperity. "Seek first the kingdom of God, and his righteousness, and all these things shall be added to you" has, among the Chols and Tzeltals, come abundantly true.

A whole countryside, its hills and valleys, has become Evangelical. Hundreds of churches have been built. About nine thousand Tzeltals are now communicant members, which means a Christian community of about 20,000, so that the tribe, which numbers about 50,000, is almost half Christian. Tzeltals speaking the Oxchuc dialect number 12,000. Of these, 6000 are full members, so the Oxchuc section of the tribe is now entirely Christian. The people movement started among the Oxchucs and spread from there. The Chols, who live just north of the Tzeltals, have a people movement of somewhat lesser size and farther to go, but are progressing well.   As among the Otomis, all pastors are of the tribe and all services are in the mother tongue.

At present there is one presbytery for the Mestizos, Chols, and Tzeltals; but indications are that three presbyteries in one Synod will suit these separate, homogeneous unit Churches better.

People movements to Christ are highly significant. True, the high people consciousness of "an Indian group" is greater than the vague people consciousness of a Mestizo countryside; but nevertheless, since each *rancho* is composed of a small number of families closely interrelated and groups of *ranchos* in one valley or section have some bonds of kinship, people movements of a qualified nature are possible throughout Mexico. If group decisions are regardel as normal, the web of relationship should enable many decisions to be made. Once they begin, they will multiply.

Therefore, many emphases of these greatly growing Indian churches can be emulated by all Churches in Mexico. All people have relatives, and the flow of the Christian faith along lines of relationship is always a sound way to proceed. "Andrew went and found his brother Simon." A leadership out of "the people being converted" — Otomi pastors for Otomis, Chol pastors for Chols — is a pattern Pentecostals use among all urban and rural populations. "Primarily spiritual, not educational, qualifications for the ministry" guarantee that the pastors will not be too far ahead of their people, as does the fact that they are paid "on an Otomi scale." (How to keep the pastors close to their people and yet far enough ahead is one of the nice problems in church growth everywhere!) Colorful Mexican forms of worship, the use of guitar, tamborine, and trumpet, and an informality which assures participation by all, can readily be duplicated by any congregation or denomination. These people movements, then, should be studied, not as exotic forms of church growth, but as Mexican forms replete with lessons for all who will learn.

10 Creating Living Connections

Church growth in Mexico faces a problem common to Churches in many parts of Africa, Asia, and Latin America. Christians have connections of a sort with their unsaved neighbors and friends, but they are not *living* connections, along which faith in Christ really flows, creating other responsible members of Evangelical churches. To put it another way, congregations and denominations get sealed off by the very redemption they possess in Christ. Their salvation separates them from their own folk. Education made possible by conversion and mission aid turns their members into persons who have less and less connection with their relatives. "Sealing off" has been mentioned several times in the previous chapters. It is a prominent part of the picture in the slow-growing Church.

Congregations get pushed into separation, too. When sinners quit worldly behavior, sorcery, drinking, and sinning, they find the world hates them. Their former co-religionists persecute them, ostracize them, and push them out of the life of the community. Separated from without and within, how can they maintain those contacts so necessary for the Christian faith to flow naturally?

Mexican converts themselves have large numbers of Roman Catholic intimates and relatives. The children and grandchildren of converts have increasingly fewer. The only Roman Catholics they know as "our own flesh and blood" are first, second and third cousins, great-uncles and great-aunts — all of whom "we seldom visit."

Connections with one's general community can, of course, be purchased at the price of conviction. Evangelicals can get connections by playing down their evangelicalism. They can marry Roman Catholics, quit being ardently Evangelical, drink, and become worldly. This will restore connection and prevent a ghetto mentality — but it will also destroy Christian faith.

How can an Evangelical community maintain good connections and ardent Evangelical faith? This is a crucial question. Be assured, close connections are necessary. A church, sealed off by persecution from without and transformation from within, literally cannot grow. The "better" it gets in terms of educational advance, cultural improvement and ethical achievement, the less chance it has to grow. It must re-establish connection. Electric current flows only where there is good connection. Even low voltage will flow where there is good connection; but high voltage is stopped dead by a gap in the line. A poor quality of Christianity will reproduce when the connections are good, while a high quality will prove sterile where genuine involvement with the community is lacking.

Christian leaders agree that good connections (involvement) are desirable. They differ on what these connections consist of and how they are created. *How,* they ask, *does a church create living contacts with its general community?* To this question the rest of the chapter is devoted.

The Otomi and Portales Churches are greatly growing denominations and will repay close study because they tell us how a Church can create connections or get involved with its community. But we must hear what they really say.

The people movement in the Otomi tribe, described in the previous chapter, has maintained connection extremely well. It has both good connections and hot sparks. It helps a new village before it evangelizes it. It meets felt needs before preaching Christ as an answer to unfelt needs.

This feature is, indeed, striking. Brother Hernandez, we recall, after his conversion waited a whole year before speaking to his Otomi laborers of Christ. During this year he was encouraging them to wear better clothes, stand up sraighter, save their money, and educate their children. He was accepted by them as genuinely interested in their welfare. When he had achieved (so it appears) a secure position as a real benefactor, then he spoke to them about the Saviour.

A pastor in Japan advocated a similar mode of evangelism. He said, "Anyone desiring to speak about Christ in Japan should not do so when he first arrives in a community. He would be scorned. He should live in it quietly, see its problems, and help it by opening a kindergarten. His wife, who might be a nurse, should start serving the community. After he has established himself as a respectable person, desiring the welfare of the community, he may then speak about Christ with some hope of being heard."

One of the great growing churches in Mexico City is the Portales congregation of the Interdenominational Pentecostal Church in a laboring community. Professor Juan Diaz, a Methodist minister and head of the Union Teological Seminary in Mexico City, says, "The Portales Church has greatly served its community. It has started co-operative credit unions and co-operative consumers' unions. It maintains a day school for its community, and has greatly helped several rural churches. It stresses a healing ministry among the common people. The service to the community rendered by this church is part of the reason for its growth."

"Ah," we say, "this is the answer. Service to the community, healing the sick, educating the illiterate, building roads to new churches, and taking the communities' burdens to our heart, create good connections. Service immerses churches in their neighborhoods and communities. It secures this precious involvement, without which the Church will not grow."

But our answer is wrong, for although the service of the Otomi and Portales churches to the community does seem to have created conditions in which the Gospel can be communicated, all across Mexico great programs of good works have been carried out by churches, missionaries, institutions and denominations without establishing "living connections." I am writing from Pabellon, Aguascalientes, where the Disciples of Christ mission and church helped a town to obtain a high school, for years contributed teachers to the staff, maintained an agricultural demonstration center, and made available to the community pedigreed bulls, better seed, and better agricultural methods. Connection of a sort was established, but "living connections," such as enable the Gospel to flow, are notably lacking. The approach recommended by the Japanese pastor has, as a matter of fact, achieved little growth in Japan. In both cases, the precious connections of intimates and relatives known a few months previously as fellow religionists do not exist.

The question must be raised, then, Which come first, good connections (involvement with the community) or good works? Do good works give birth to involvement, or does involvement give birth to good works? When a church membership is well connected with its community, does it *then* see things to do?

In the case of the Otomis, it is certain that good connections existed long before the good works began. In the Otomi tribe, everyone is bound together by a common language, culture, *ejidos,* and a web of relationship caused by long-practiced endogamy. Vernancio Hernandez, partly because he was indwelt by Christ and partly because he was a good Otomi in intimate relationship with hundreds of other Otomis, was an effective discipler and a servant of his tribe. Service was, indeed, one good way to approach a new village; but the Gospel could, we surmise, have been communicated without this service approach, as the even more spectacular growth of the Church among the Tseltals and Chols indicates. Building roads to new churches was a beautiful Christian act, as well as an intelligent one. The road must have caused much comment favorable to the Christian faith. All this is true, but abundant proclamation of the Gospel in his responsive tribe, already knit together, would probably have produced church growth without building roads, as it has in hundreds of people movements in all parts of the world, not specially noted for service.

In the case of the Portales Church (a part of the Iglesia Interdenominational with its 500 congregations and preaching points throughout Mexico), Dr. Eugene Nida of the Bible Society says that it exists primarily for the sake of mission. "This intensely organized church, under the leadership of a group of lay pastors, has a job for every member, with a special concentration on visitation and invitation of people to the church and with constant follow-up and a 'big-brother-in-Christ' program *to guarantee the spiritual training and growth of new members.* [Italics mine.] This church, despite its origin in one of the poorest sections of Mexico City, is appealing increasingly to a high class of individuals, with the result that its leadership is of unusual capacity and its potential ministry almost unlimited."

The fact must be emphasized that a membership composed of new converts (which the Portales Church has) already has a vast number of excellent connections. In Mexico City men and women becoming Evangelicals do not meet severe ostracism, economic boycott, and personal harassment. Few Portalisites are second-generation Christians. They are converts and have not passed through the transforming and separating process of growing up in Evangelical churches and schools. The program of service carried on by the Portales Church has no doubt helped spread the Faith. It has given the new converts something to talk about with pride. It has given the church standing in the community and increased he number of good connections.

It would be an error to reason, however, from the experience of the Otomi and Portales Churches, that a *sealed-off* congregation could start co-operative credit societies, day schools, kindergartens, and dispensaries, and create enough "living connections" to start growing. Something much more intimate and costly is required.

The true answer to the problem of "involvement with community" and "living connections with unconverted society" lies in a different direction. The true answer is this: By every way possible, by great concern for the unsaved, by identification with the Seeking, Finding Saviour, men and women must be won to Christ and added to His Church. Many new churches must be started. As this takes place, weak connections will multiply and grow strong. The living web of relationship will be recreated. The Church will cease to be a fellowship of those converted long ago, or born Evangelicals. It will become a fellowship of converts, each with many close connections with the world. Each one will be able to say, "I, too, my brother, stood where you now stand. I know the burden you bear. Christ healed me of the very sickness which afflicts you. Trust Him. Confess Him before men. Be baptized in His name. Work and rejoice in His Church. Believe me, it is wonderful."

A rapidly growing church has connections — thousands of them. Under some circumstances, it will "serve its community," enhance these connections, and show the compassion of Christ. Under other circumstances, it will do what Paul in Corinth did — simply preach Christ crucified, and add to the church the people who believe and entrust their lives to Him. Corinthian Christians "created in Christ for good works" doubtless were better neighbors and friends than they had ever been before. But if the Apostle used philanthropy as a means to "create community" with those to whom he was sent, we have no record of it in the New Testament.

What shall we say, then, concerning the multitudinous good deeds by Christian missions through schools, hospitals, centers and farms, which in many places throughout the world have been a means of breaking down prejudice, creating friends, getting a hearing for the Gospel, and winning converts? A few years ago, in Nigeria, I asked a class of seventh-grade boys how many of them had parents who were Christian. Eight raised their hands. I then asked, "How many of you are Christian?" All 43 boys in the class raised their hands. The Seventh-Day Adventist Church in the Philippines has been doubling every eight or ten years. When in Manila I asked its head to what human factors he ascribed this growth. He replied, "Our hospitals and schools play a very important part in this growth."

The fact is that under some circumstances, in some lands,

in the hands of some Churches and some missions, connections created by mission institutions do lead to a constant stream of conversions. Under other circumstances, in other lands, and in the hands of other churchmen or missionaries, philanthropic institutions create thousands of connections, out of which only a very few persons become responsible members of the Church. Sometimes none do. This meager outcome should not be confused with "the constant stream."

In Mexico we know of no institutional approach which leads to anything more than an occasional convert. And it is our considered opinion that the great growth of the Otomi and Portales Churches cannot be ascribed primarily to their programs of good works. These undoubtedly help, but "the living connections" are of much greater significance.

How shall we establish living connections? How shall we achieve the involvement of a church with its community? The fundamental answer is by continuous, costly, and Spirit-directed *finding of the lost*. Churches with rapid growth have good connections. They have *inevitable, unsought involvement* with their communities. Encirclement (such as we described in the first paragraphs of this chapter) to them is no problem. They break out of every encirclement before it can become binding. No one can seal them off. Before a convert is transformed so far that he is separated, he has led several others to Christ, and they, in turn, are leading still others. If the number of converts is large enough, church growth of a new magnitude results. Not only are there more converts, but there is a new kind of church growth.

With connections aplenty, it is good for any church to serve its community. Our Lord commanded it. The Christian Church everywhere has served men. New Christians become more humane in all their contacts with men and women and children. Christ in the heart makes disciples good servants. This, too, should be emphasized.

With connections aplenty, it is good for any church to engage in social action — in its neighborhood, town, and nation. God works out His purposes for men, in part at least, through His Church. The crying ills of today require redress. The chains of oppression, serfdom, ignorance, and drink must be broken. Most social action depends on Christians for implementation. Christ in the heart leads men to crusade for justice, peace, and plenty for everyone. This, too, should be emphasized.

But a static Church should substitute neither good deeds nor Christian action for "adding multitudes to the Lord." Nor should it imagine that either deeds or action will of themselves bring men to belief.

An interesting instance of cultural overhang is seen in the current emphasis on involvement and is germane to this chapter. Lack of involvement is a marked characteristic of the Churches of the West, particularly of Europe. One commonly hears that the Church has become irrelevant. The 1952 diagnosis of Emmanual Suhard, a French Cardinal of the Roman Catholic Church, is typical. He writes as follows, "The Church has not evolved with civil society. She has remained frozen in feudal forms which worked in times past. In our time, instead of being fused with society as she was in the middle ages when the parish and the commune had the same extension and the same life, the Church is "absent" from the city. She hovers over humanity instead of being incarnate in its flesh and blood. . . . She lets strangers, or adversaries, take the decisive initiative on questions of doctrine, culture or action. When she acts or speaks, it is often too late. In scientific research, social legislation, or humanism she has few innovators. . . . She must become incarnate."[1]

European Protestants also lament that the Church has become irrelevant. The masses pass the Church by. It simply does not count with them any more. It has retreated into its institutions. Vicars and pastors preach in large churches to a few dozens. In like vein, the American John C. Bennett writes, "It is perhaps the most fateful fact in the history of

1 Emmanuel Suhard, *The Church Today; Growth or Decline?* (Fides Publishers, 1960).

modern Europe that the working people and the democratic forces in Europe came to believe that the Church was against them."

In the West, in general, the remedy usually prescribed is some form of Cardinal Suhard's dictum: "The Church must become incarnate." This is a most popular emphasis in Europe and in parts of America today. The Church must be related to all of life. She must become involved in the life of the common people. She must serve men more. She must get into politics. Christians must know what is the Christian position in regard to the great issues of this day and vote for them. Christians must run for public office on a Christian platform. The ghetto mentality must be avoided at all costs. Pietism must be renounced for social action.

This may be a correct diagnosis for Europe where the churches — Protestant and Roman Catholic — still have enormous power, where Christians if they would but exert themselves could change society, and where there are enough Christians to make involvement pay off. In Europe "involvement" might make the Church grow in numbers and be the key to its survival. But, although involvement is beneficial to the Church in Europe, is that reason to believe it will be beneficial to the Churches in Mexico?

The sealed-off nature of hundreds of tiny Protestant churches in Mexico is not at all like that of the great Churches in Europe. Social action by Churches of five million members whose votes will swing elections and whose ablest men can run for office and get elected is something far different from social action by little bands of scorned Protestants in fanatical towns. The current, much publicized medicine in Europe is not likely to cure "the sealed-offness" of these little bands. Much more effective will be the involvement which comes as an unsought dividend of a continuous stream of converts.

11 The Pentecostal Contribution

A large share of the increased opportunity for Evangelical advance is due to the phenomenal growth of the Pentecostal denominations — small in Mexico compared with Brazil and Chile, but very large compared with most other Mexican Churches.

Up to the present, however, many denominations have shut themselves off from this opportunity by their judgment that Pentecostals are a highly irregular and unstable kind of Evangelicals.

In 1919 Pentecostals started in Chile. By 1930 they numbered 10,000. In that year the authors of *West Coast Republics* (the best survey of churches and missions in Peru, Chile and Bolivia until 1962 when Keith Hamilton's *Church Growth in the High Andes* was published) quoted "a well-informed correspondent" who declared that the Pentecostal movement "has now probably reached its climax and no gains have been made in recent years. . . . In a short time the field will have been burned over and the movement die down. This would appear all the more certain from the fact that its methods do not hold young people, most of whom are intellectually in advance of their parents."

Mark Twain once said, "The report of my death has been slightly exaggerated." The Pentecostals of Chile might well say the same. They now number 200,000 full members and are beginning to attract men and women of the middle classes.

Bishop Newbigin of the United Church of South India has said somewhere, "If any Church believes in the deity of Jesus Christ and the authority of the Bible and manifests the fruits of the Spirit, we are on dangerous grounds to question its validity." By that standard each Pentecostal

113

denomination is a sound Church indeed! Continued Pentecostal growth forces old-line denominations to consider
whether the Pentecostals may not have a valuable contribution to make. Should we not recognize in the Pentecostal
denominations one of God's rich gifts to His Universal
Church?

Under the guidance of the Holy Spirit Himself — no man
planned this — the Pentecostal denominations have found a
way out if the impasse into which many Branches of the
Church have come. Pentecostals have grown with a minimum
of "mission money" and in some cases with none at all. They
have largely avoided both the national-missionary tension and
the interminable discussion of national-missionary and church-
mission relationship, which in some quarters today passes for
Christian mission.

What, then, is this way? What is the Pentecostal
contribution?

Its most prominent belief is that God Himself, through
the Holy Spirit, personally guides and directs each disciple
of Christ, granting him power to overcome inner temptations
and outer assaults; and that the gift of this Power is normally
made known to the believer by a joyful, shattering experience, in which he sometimes "speaks in tongues," weeps, or
gives other physical expression to his overwhelming feelings.
Pentecostals count as full members believers who accept the
first baptism (of water). All these then are expected to pray
for, wait for, and receive the second baptism (of the Holy
Spirit). Many of them receive it.

Just as the Holy Spirit causes believers to speak in an
unpredictable fashion, so He will also lead them to do what
"seems good to the Holy Spirit" (see James and the Jeru-
salem Council of the year 54). He will send Christians to
preach. He will give them power to persuade. He will heal
at their hands, and give heed to their prayer. Christians are
not bound to "mission tradition." They are free to do what
in their circumstances seems good to them — to what *in their
circumstances* the Holy Spirit commands. The principle of

spontaneous action under the control of the Spirit of Jesus as revealed in the Scriptures lies at the heart of the Pentecostal faith. Anything which the situation requires is permissible — provided the Holy Spirit (the same Person who acted in the New Testament) approves.

This principle — or shall we more truly say the Holy Spirit — has blasted a way through five tremendous roadblocks in the path of Christian mission, exactly as He did through the 20-year conviction which until A.D. 50 confined the Gospel to the Jews.

The first roadblock was that Evangelical Churches in Mexico received long years of tutelage, support, educational aid, and guidance by the "Mission." This tradition is common all around the world. Younger Churches are supposed to have, even in these latter days, decades of "partnership in obedience" during which they work together with older churches. Old-line denominations seldom plant a Church and really let it go. Their assistance to it grows with every passing decade. If they diminish the number of missionaries they send it, they increase the number of dollars.

In sharp contradistinction is the experience of most Pentecostal denominations. La Iglesia Apostolica de la Fe en Cristo Jesus is typical of them. In 1916 a laborer from Mexico was converted in a Pentecostal meeting in the United States; he returned to Mexico, preached Christ to his fellows, and led many of them to decision. As a layman, he felt he could not baptize them, and so he invited an American minister to come down and baptize. The American did this and returned to America, leaving the new church with Scriptures and the Holy Spirit in true apostolic fashion. That 1916 beginning has by 1962 grown to a denomination of 9000[1] full members, over 100 ordained ministers, and with church buildings costing to date at least 1,000,000 *pesos*. It has had no missionaries and little, if any, financial assistance from the States. It and its sister denomination in the United States

1 Some of its ministers say 30,000.

jointly support 20 Mexican missionaries in other parts of Latin America. Under the direction of the Holy Spirit, this tremendous new departure, which many old-line denominations labor to achieve, has quietly come about. Mission tutelage and support neither occurred nor continued.

The second roadblock avoided was insatiable, *unrelated* institutionalism. In the process of planting churches, many Christian missions build up large institutions, begun for all kinds of good reasons, to do all kinds of good deeds. These institutions help the public, help the younger Church, are indirectly evangelistic, give the Evangelical cause prestige — and they gradually use up larger and larger proportions of missionaries, budgets, nationals, and attention. They are insatiable. They attract able missionaries, and from them are chosen many of the executives of mission boards. The missionaries want them, the nationals want them, the boards want them, and the sending Churches love them. They appear to be an absolutely essential part of Christian mission. They divert a very large proportion of mission resources (cash and men) to excellent work which has only a slight connection with reconciling men to God.

We are not here speaking of institutions genuinely related to growing Churches. The theological training school of a Church of 30,000 communicants is essential to its welfare. A teacher-training college in the Congo (where the denomination of 125,000 communicants maintains all the schools necessary for the education of a population of 300,000) is related to church growth and is essential. We are not speaking of "insatiable institutions" but of "insatiable *unrelated* institutions."

The Pentecostals walked through this roadblock without even seeing it. Their function was to win men to Christ and to plant churches, and this they did. They had no money for auxiliary institutions, no trained missionaries to establish them, and did not see the need for them. Their church was for them hospital, social center, educational plant, and sanctuary. We do not argue that their total neglect of institutions (except for Bible training schools) is always sound procedure; but *in responsive populations* Pentecostals have demonstrated that churches can grow (as they did in New Testament times) without institutional assistance. They have also demonstrated that *in responsive populations* churches grow better when they center attention on the Church.

One is reminded of Peter Cartwright's formula for a Methodist preacher. He said, "A Methodist preacher, when he felt that God had called him to preach, instead of hunting up a college or biblical institute, hunted up a hardy pony and some traveling apparatus, and set forth. With Bible, hymn book, and Discipline always at hand, and a text that never wore out or grew stale, he cried, 'Behold the Lamb of · God, who takes away the sin of the world!' "

The third roadblock was denationalization. It was difficult for missionaries to plant churches without making them carbon copies of their own in their homeland. Middle-class denominations from America had a tradition of beautiful, orderly worship. This was how — they believed — God should be worshiped, and they led their younger Churches to worship in this way. Leading Churches established seminaries in which they strove to reach the standards of their seminaries in the United States or England. If Barth was studied in New Jersey, he should be studied in Mexico. Mexican ministers should have the *same* high standards that Americans had. These "cultural overhangs" were largely unconscious and were put into effect, whether the Church grew or not. If a more effective way of planting churches had been pointed out to church leaders, they would have replied, "Quite impossible. That is just not the way our denomination is accustomed to do."

The Pentecostal denominations blew this roadblock up before they reached it. Converts were free "in the Spirit" to adopt any procedure not contrary to the mind of Christ. They had little missionary guidance or denomination. They were for the most part men and women of the masses, and they proceeded to do what men and women of the masses

liked. As Roman Catholics, they had been accustomed to
going up to the chancel to pray, or to kneel in their pews
and pray before leaving the church. And this they continued
to do. In the Roman Catholic churches they had been accustomed to praying their own prayers each to himself in a
whisper, in the solitude of a vast nave. This they continued
to do, but out loud in their joyful Pentecostal fellowship.
The vast volume of sound rushing up to God, the complete
secrecy of such prayer, and the gentle pressure to participate
seemed good to them, and there were no missionaries to tell
them that this was disorderly, undignified, and that it dis-
credited Evangelicals. Pentecostals were not afraid of being
undignified. They were indigenous by birth. Their songs,
prayers, churches, pastors, guitars, and cymbals all came in
without strain. They simply transplanted Mexico into their
churches.

The fourth roadblock in the way of traditional Christian
mission (and a very tough one) is the self-support of the
ministry. Most missions started out paying evangelists from
mission funds — a highly sensible thing to do. As converts
were won, evangelists become pastors. Their salaries were
shifted over on to the church. That was the theory. It seldom
worked, except where the churches multiplied enormously
in some people movement to Christ. Missions could not cut
off mission subsidy without great pain and some loss. All
around the world younger Churches and their assisting missions are constantly engaged in campaigns of "stewardship"
and "self-support," trying desperately to get churches to
support their own ministers. And with some degree of success,
too. But "adequate ministerial training" continually makes
the task more difficult. Highly trained ministers are upper
class ministers and command upper-class salaries. Yet, they
must be supported by Christians of the masses.

In 1942 Merle Davis of the International Missionary
Council wrote some words about Brazil which apply to
Mexico also. "The rural community in Brazil is living close
to the subsistence level. The appearance in their midst of

a family of non-producers [the minister's] whom they must support [at a middle-class level] is a disaster."[2] (Insertions mine.)

The Pentecostals walked around this one. They early determined that their qualifications for the ministry were spiritual, not educational. If a person could lead a church to grow in grace and manifest a divine compassion to reconcile men to God in Christ, Pentecostals judged that man a pastor, appointed not by men, but by God. Men are eager to know if there is a power which can save them from their sins, cleanse them, hold them from falling back into sin, and help them to know and find God. Men will listen to this kind of Gospel. The Pentecostal pastors can preach this Gospel effectively because they are just like other men, are not separated from them by clericalism, and have been saved.

"The Pentecostal churches," said Merle Davis in 1942, "have evolved a practical leadership and a simple message that are suited to the task of evangelizing the masses of Brazil. The pastors come from the humble class and are given a series of institute training courses, usually alternating periods of preaching with periods of study. . . . Simplicity of pastoral training is also adapted to a rapidly expanding movement. Many small congregations are not left without leadership . . . humble leaders can live upon an economic level impossible for highly trained men."[3]

Dr. Eugene Nida in 1962 wrote,

> In the most indigenous Churches, leaders are normally trained by informal educational methods and primarily through apprenticeship systems. In some indigenous Churches in Mexico, for example, a congregation which has grown to the size of 50 to 100 members under the tutelage of another church is always encouraged to elect a local person as a "pastor," who is then ordained by leaders of the movement and authorized

2 Merle Davis, *How the Church Grows in Brazil* (International Missionary Council, 1943), p. 68.
3 *Ibid.*, p. 84.

to administer the sacraments. This local pastor is often the best educated person in the congregation, but the principal qualifications are spiritual, not intellectual. Once he has been appointed, however, he is expected to gather with other pastors once a week or once a month for a period of Bible study, prayer, fasting, and discussion of church plans and programs. Also, he is encouraged to attend frequent conferences of the churches, where he continues to learn more about how to preach, what to teach, and how to organize and develop his church. His salary depends on the extent to which the local group wants to support him, so as to make possible his frequent travel and the portion of his time he must take from his work as farmer, carpenter, or mason to give to the church.

By selecting pastors from the community in which they are to minister it is not only possible to develop leadership on a viable economic basis, but such persons are likely to be much more faithful within their own communities than if they were sent into a new area, where the social pressures would not be so great for conforming their lives to the new standards they have openly espoused. Moreover, a man who has lived for years within a community has no problem in knowing the people or understanding their problems.[4]

Pentecostals also emphasize tithing. Their churches preach tithing. New Christians come into a fellowship where many are already tithing. Their large churches pay their pastors well. Their small churches pay very much less to men of small education who are often only part-time preachers. With a movement usually strongly national and independent of a mission board, they find that they can do what mission churches think is quite impossible. So the roadblock of "self-support" has been effectively by-passed.

The fifth roadblock traditional missions have run into

4 Eugene Nida, An unpublished manuscript at The Institute of Church Growth, Eugene, Oregon.

— and which has grown higher with th⌐ ⌐   ⌐ is the resistance of the classes.

Early converts were often men and women who read ⌐ie Bible and drew the inevitable conclusion that Roman Catholicism is not the religion of Jesus Christ and His apostles. Only literates could read the Bible, and only highly intelligent literates could form such a conclusion from it. Thus some early converts were exceptional persons of the classes.

Many missionaries also — particularly those who took up the service approach through colleges and schools — interpreted their task as the evangelization of the classes, and to this end, sought warm, personal relationships with the classes.

Despite these warm, personal relationships and the avid desire of the classes for English education, in Latin America the classes have had a four-century alliance with the Church of Rome. Latin America was ruled by an economic-social-political-Roman Catholic block. Even when members of this block became anti-clerical, because they resented the political power and control of the Roman Catholic Church, they did not renounce the Church or reform it. They merely sought to curb its political power. They had too many economic, social and cultural ties with their Church for them to leave it.

Thus many Evangelical missions fell into a vicious circle. To present the Gospel at all to the cultured classes, they established warm, personal friendships on the basis of Christian service. To keep the friendships warm, they were careful not to present the Gospel too aggressively. And, since their time was used up approaching and serving the business and professional people of the city, who were by nature resistant and not obedient to the Gospel, they had little time left to press the claims of Christ on the vast, neglected, and by nature responsive masses.

The alleged "responsiveness of the masses" must be understood. As long as they were in the grip of the upper classes — as *peons* on *haciendas,* servants, or wage slaves in factories owned by the upper classes — they appeared more resistant than these classes themselves. They believed the priests implicitly — four hundred years had taught them it was wise to do so! They obediently tore up Bibles and threw stones at Evangelicals. The *Cristeros* show how firm the grip of the classes was on the masses. In the Cristero Movement of 1927, the priests and land owners actually persuaded their landless serfs that distribution of the *hacendados'* land was stealing, forbidden by God Himself, and if done would bring down a curse on the people of the land. Even today in high central Mexico many peasants believe that the recent years of drought are God's curse on godless land distributors.

But wherever the masses achieved economic freedom, they became more or less responsive. They were Roman Catholics, not by conviction but by inheritance, ignorance and manipulation. When they reached a place where the priest could no longer manipulate or the *hacendado* drive them out of employment, house and home, the religious vacuum of their lives welcomed Christ.

Factory cities (especially where the factories were owned by Americans), government employment (for the revolutionary government was committed to breaking the political power of the Roman Catholic Church), border towns, revolutionary *ranchos,* remote mountain valleys, hot, swampy coastal plains, and new settlements — in all these the masses were somewhat free to accept Christ.

These were the very places from which traditional missions (by their early converts from the classes, their American middle-classness, their educated predilections, the bias of their institutions toward the business and professional people of the city and, it must be added, their second- and third-generation Evangelicals who had grown up into the middle class and valued their status) were shut out.

This was a roadblock which the Pentecostals did not encounter at all. Their first converts were — almost inevitably — free people of the masses. These worked among the only people they knew — their own kinsmen. The web of relationship along which Christianity flows led surely to the responsive among the masses. The Pentecostal churches began and continued to be churches of the masses — frankly, unashamedly, and to a great degree unintentionally so.

Because the day of the masses had come, as men became disciples of Christ in Pentecostal denominations, they were redeemed by Christ, found solid jobs at good wages in railways, government departments and neutral factories. They prospered. They had started out as tithers. As their income rose, so did that of their churches. Pentecostal church buildings are often beautiful and adequate — and paid for by Mexican citizens.

The Pentecostal march to the promised land did not encounter the resistant classes. We believe the Holy Spirit led them by a better way and is through them showing that way to traditional missions and Churches.

The suppressed experience of most traditional Evangelical denominations confirms the responsiveness of the masses. Despite some outstanding converts from the upper classes, most converts in all Evangelical churches have come from the lower classes. Despite the fact that many old-line missionaries worked openly and unashamedly for the conversion of the classes, despite the theory that the correct approach in Latin America started with winning the anti-clerical classes, the overwhelming response has come from the masses. One is reminded of India[5] where so many missionaries worked for the upper castes and God led into His Church hundreds of thousands of the so-called Untouchables. The Bible also tells us that when the Church began in Corinth, Christ being preached by the incomparable Paul, God chose the foolish, the weak, and the "things which are not" to put to shame the wise, the strong and the things which are.

It may well be in Mexico, as it has proved in India, that strong churches of the common people will present Christ more effectively to their neighbors of the middle and upper

5 Read J. W. Pickett's "Christ's Way to India's Heart," available from the Institute of Church Growth.

classes than highly trained North Americans using all kinds of "indirect evangelism."

In India, Bishop J. W. Pickett discovered that the only places where considerable numbers of the upper castes were becoming Christian were where the depressed classes in great numbers had espoused Christ and been transformed in life. The beneficiaries of the social order seldom move first. Why should they? They "have it too good." But when the victims of the social order become Christian, they not only are redeemed but also open the way for the privileged classes (living in their midst and dependent on them for labor, and other social necessities) to accept Christ.

Many full-time missionaries to Indian Moslems, becoming experts in Islamics and in Arabic, have devoted a lifetime to presenting Christ to Moslems. Yet their converts can be numbered on the fingers of one hand. Pickett points out that where in the Punjab the landless laborers as a whole became Christian, many Moslems (living in their midst and dependent on them) observed the changed life and slowly, one here and another there, became Christian.

Mexico is not India and Roman Catholic society is not the caste system, yet it may be that the common people are Christ's way to Mexico's heart. At any rate, there are many of them in the *ranchos,* the *pueblos,* and the *ciudades,* and many of them are responsive.

The emergence of true middle classes in Mexico introduces a new and encouraging factor, especially since these middle classes rise from the bottom. As multitudes of common people become sincere disciples of Christ, He will redeem them body and soul. The Pentecostals in Chile are finding that their second and third generations are rising into the middle classes and through them other members of the middle classes are finding Christ in the Pentecostal churches.

12　The Puzzle of Mexico Reviewed

This preliminary study of church growth has probed the growth of Evangelical Churches in Mexico. The historical findings are briefly summarized below in five periods.

(1) Before 1857, Mexico was a typical Roman Catholic possession, deliberately and effectively sealed off against all forms of Protestantism. Both the difficulties of getting into Mexico and the slight awareness of Evangelical Churches in North America and Europe of their missionary obligations prevented any missionary movement and any establishment of Evangelical congregations.

(2) Between the Juarez revolution of 1857 and 1880, little was accomplished for several reasons, one of which was the small number of Evangelicals determined enough to establish churches in Mexico.

Prof. Gonzalo Baez Camargo of the American Bible Society says that during these years many priests left the Roman Catholic Church. Filled with pro-Juarez sentiments, some wished to form a Mexican Catholic Church and others independent Catholic churches. If Protestantism had been aware of this opportunity and welcomed these priests, many would have come, with their entire congregations, into the Protestant fold. But as time went on, their loosely knit organization broke up and many fell back into the Roman Catholic Church. A few became Presbyterians and Methodists, but the times were not propitious. The foreign missions of these two North American Churches were not strong enough to seize the opportunity. Perhaps they did not see it clearly. The Civil War in the United States intervened. At any rate, this period went by without any real beginning of growth.

125

(3) From 1880 to 1910 several missions entered Mexico, many people accepted the Lord Jesus, and many Evangelical churches were established. Indeed, the large denominational boards all met with considerable success. The Congregational Church had 1500 members in 1910 — to be compared with 600 from 1930 to 1960. The Christian Church (Disciples of Christ) had 900 in 9 churches in 1908, and did not get back to this figure until 1961.

(4) Period Four lasted from 1911 to 1936. The revolutionary times and anti-church laws handicapped the older missions. A comity arrangement prevented overlapping, but at the same time separated some congregations from their supporting boards, introduced a good deal of bitterness, and divided Protestant missions into old-line co-operators and new-line intruders. These factors added up to 25 years of disaster for the missions which arrived in Mexico before 1906. From 23,000, the members of their Churches declined to 22,000, as is seen in the following tables.

The figures taken from the 1910 and 1938 Surveys,[1] representing the memberships about 1908 and 1936, proclaim 25 "very difficult" years.

BOARDS	1910 COMMUNICANTS	1938 COMMUNICANTS
Methodist	12,470	10,300
Presbyterian	5,700	5,300
Congregational	1,540	600
Friends	670	200
Christian Churches	900	600
American Baptists	1,202	3,440
Southern Baptists	1,428	2,442
	23,910	22,882

1 *World Atlas of Christian Missions and Interpretative Statistical Survey.*

The missions and Churches which came to Mexico after 1906, however, have a strikingly different picture.

	1910 COMMUNICANTS	1938 COMMUNICANTS
Mexican Indian	0	560
Assemblies of God	0	6,000
Adventists	70	4,000
Pentecostal Holiness	0	1,300
Pilgrim Holiness	0	1,200
Nazarenes	0	2,000
Swedish Pentecostal	0	4,000
	70	19,060

In the 25 "very difficult" years, these newer boards and Churches had added 19,060 communicants to the Church of Christ in Mexico. This occurred in spite of the turbulent revolutionary years, their own inexperience, Roman Catholic fanaticism, and the disfavor with which they were viewed by the older Evangelical missions!

To these 19,060 must be added the beginnings of the Iglesia Apostolica de la Fe en Cristo Jesus, the Interdenominational Pentecostal Church famed for the Portales Church, the Independent Evangelical (Pentecostal) Church, the Church of God fathered by the Los Angeles Four Square Gospel Church, and others. The combined memberships of these Churches by 1936 numbered at least 6,000, so that the total new growth during this "very difficult period" was likely in excess of 25,000 full members.

The graph "A Strange Outcome" vividly illustrates the contrast. For the "New Boards" only the figures given in the 1938 Interpretative Statistical Survey published by the International Missionary Council are used. If the additional 6,000 members, mentioned in the paragraph above, were added, the graph would be still more striking.

This fourth period has crucial significance for Christian mission. It bristles with questions concerning mission policies. It seem to refute many cherished axioms concerning

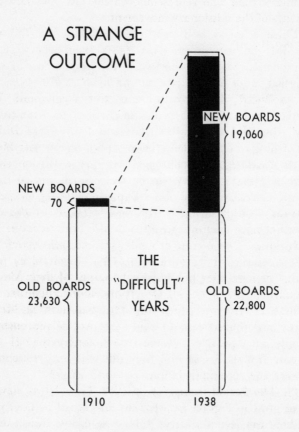

A STRANGE
OUTCOME

NEW BOARDS
19,060

NEW BOARDS
70

THE
"DIFFICULT"
YEARS

OLD BOARDS
23,630

OLD BOARDS
22,800

1910   1938

"sound" procedure. It should be most carefully studied by missionary scholars who rid themselves of promotional bias and denominational pride, who have access to the archives of several different mission boards, and who consult many men and women who represent both the fast- and slow-growing wings of the missionary movement.

These scholars will ask questions like the following. Why did the newcomers gain 25,000 members while the major boards, with the enormous advantage of a thirty-year head start, were declining from 23,000 to 22,000? What policies produced this growth — and this stagnation? Were Christian leaders conscious of the disaster, or were they so "busy" they did not realize what was happening? Did the years of decline make these missions more ardent that Mexico be won to Christ, or did these years cause missionaries to believe the real task in Mexico was "quiet service in the name of Christ"? How did the Baptists partially escape this disastrous "consolidation"? Did some sections of the older missions achieve great church growth and other sections great church loss? If so, were growing sections reinforced? Did board secretaries in America accept the "inevitability of no growth," or were they helpless in the hands of their Mexican missionaries? Among the various commissions appointed during these 25 years to study the Christian task in Mexico, was any one commanded to study this loss of movement in the midst of populations where it was unnecessary? If "no," why not? If "yes," what did they find out and recommend, and were the recommendations put into effect?

(5) The Period from 1936 to 1962. First, let us view the facts of growth. Figures for 1962 are combined in the following table from several sources. Like most figures from younger Churches, they are approximations, yet have a rough correspondence with reality. *World Christian Handbook* figures for 1962 have been corrected by those furnished by Rev. Gustavo Velasco in August, 1962. They are as reliable as any now available. All figures given are for the category variously named full members, baptized believers, or communicants.

BOARDS	1910	1938	1962
Methodist	12,470	10,300	33,000
Presbyterian	5,700	5,300	42,000
Congregational	1,540	600	600
Friends	670	200	100
Christian	900	600	1,000
American Baptists	1,202	3,440	5,000
Southern Baptists	1,428	2,442	7,640
Mexican Indian	0	560	6,000
Assemblies I & II	0	6,000	15,000
Adventists	70	4,000	22,700
Pentecostal Holiness	0	1,300	—
Pilgrim Holiness	0	1,200	5,700
Nazarene	0	2,000	5,700
Swedish Pentecostals	0	4,000	15,000
Indian Apostolic	0	—	9,000
Church of God (Four Sq.)	0	—	10,000
Churches of God (US & Prophecy)	0	—	15,500
Interdenominational	0	—	27,000
Miepi	0	—	10,000
Others	0	—	40,000

Period Five lasted about 25 years — remembering that the 1938 figures were actually those for 1936. This second 25-year period reveals much growth. The decline of the Methodists and Presbyterians ends. The former increased threefold and the latter eightfold. Southern Baptists increased about threefold, most of the increase being registered in the last decade. The other Baptists and Christian Churches chalk up minor increases. The United Church of Christ (Congregational) is at a standstill, as are the Friends.

All the missions which entered Mexico after 1906 have grown, but there are clearly two categories. Those growing moderately (less than threefold increases) include the Assemblies of God I and II, the Nazarenes, and the Swedish Pentecostals.[2] Those growing greatly include the Mexican Indian, the Adventists, Iglesia Apostolica de la Fe en Cristo

---

2 This may not be fair to the Swedish Pentecostals. Velasco gives them 15,000 members — but *World Christian Handbook* gives them 50,000 and the 4000 figure of 1936 given by Interpretative Statistical Survey may be high or low. The Swedish Pentecostals are now compiling responsible figures and we shall know the facts in a year or two.

Jesus, Church of God I and II, Miepi, and Interdenominational Church (Portales).

Considering early and late comers together, we may say that eightfold growth of the Presbyterians, fivefold growth of the Adventists, elevenfold growth of the Mexican Indian Mission, and the exceedingly rapid increase of the Apostolics, Churches of God, and Interdenominational (Portales) Church are noteworthy. They prove that rapid growth is not the prerogative of any one kind of Church. Any of the missions and Churches at work in Mexico could have had notable church growth if they had wanted it enough to pay the price for it. If they had gone where God had prepared for Himself a people, proclaimed the Gospel so that it could be heard and obeyed, avoided the roadblocks we mentioned in Chapter 10, taken advantage of "people movement" insights, and constantly checked their theories, locations, budget distributions, and activities against the degree of church growth granted them by God, they would have grown.

Some populations intentionally and decisively reject Jesus Christ the Lord. When the Gospel is proclaimed to these, churches do not grow. Some Mexican populations are of this character, but we are not speaking about them. Scattered in amongst these rebellious and resistant populations are individuals, groups, webs of families which can become disciples of Christ. It is these latter who destroy the comfortable illusion that "we are doing all we can possibly do in this impossibly difficult field." Much lack of church growth is remediable. It is of this we speak.

* * *

The major causes of church growth have been discussed throughout this book. They are summarized in the following paragraphs in the way of re-emphasis and clarification.

The Indwelling Christ must be present in the hearts of missionaries, ministers, and Christians. If Christ is not there, His Body will not grow. His churches will not multiply. The

Holy Spirit of God is an absolute necessity. He it is who uses the following factors.

An indefinitely reproduceable pattern of congregations is an essential factor. Church growth occurs where each congregation, as fast as it becomes established, without undue dependence on outside guidance or financial resources, can go ahead planting other churches like itself.

The use of ordained men, not too far in advance of the laymen, recompensed at a level possible to the members, recruited from among those becoming Christian, and constantly engaged in finding lost sheep, is another factor of great significance.

Laymen, unpaid and fairly recently converted, who manifest the new life in Christ and who actively seek to save others and lead their churches, are a potent factor in church growth. The church must be theirs. They must have such a large part in it, and it must be so obviously Christ's Church, that they never think of it as "belonging to" the ministers or missionaries.

Responsive segments of the population are essential to church growth. The Spirit of God still broods over the hearts of men, preparing His chosen people to follow Moses out of Egypt. In Mexico His "people" may live in certain *ranchos* or *pueblos;* they may be factory workers or *braceros;* or they may be members of one or another tribe. Churches grow which consciously or unconsciously find these responsive populations.

A self-image conducive to growth is desirable. Churches multiply which think of themselves as indwelt by the Saviour and commanded by the Lord who wants His banquet hall filled. Churches multiply if they believe it is their primary task to grow. A church whose self-image is that of a kindly group of people, establishing friendships with people like themselves and doing good to others, is unlikely to win converts in any substantial number. A church that thinks its duty complete in fellowshiping with leading business and professional people in its cities cannot multiply.

"People-movement" principles are conducive to church growth. Where a Christward movement spreads from person to person in such a fashion that related individuals decide for Christ in consultation with each other, and then spread the light to others in their web of relationship, a people movement to Christ develops. This involves both individual and multi-individual conversion along the lines of family and tribal relationships.

The maintenance of "living connections" between Christians and people of the world is a prerequisite for major church growth. Nothing produces these connections more effectively than a constant stream of conversions from "the world." Conversions from within the Evangelical fold, desirable as they are, do not produce connections with the outside. This is why it is so dangerous to allow or encourage stoppage in church growth. To "stop and consolidate" is detrimental under all circumstances and fatal under some. Good connections can be produced by artificial means — identification, good works, imagination — but nothing takes the place of the unsought, natural, living connections of recent converts.

The above is not an exhaustive list. Other causes of church growth will be discerned both in the previous chapters of this book and, even more, as Christians look for them among the growing and non-growing sections of the Evangelical Church in Mexico.

Denominations which discover, welcome, and follow such principles of action will be those through which Christ works to the redemption of many. The future belongs to Churches which grow. No Church worthy of the name wants to grow in order to be large and powerful; but every Church worthy of the name wants to grow in order that "as grace extends to more and more people, it may increase thanksgiving, to the glory of God."

We trust that as readers come to the end of this volume they will have more questions about church growth than they had at the beginning. The puzzle of church growth in

Mexico is not solved, but it has been laid open for all to see. More research by scholars on what has really been happening is urgent. To deal with Mexico adequately, they will need to become competent in church growth principles through studying how churches have and have not grown in many places throughout the earth. They will then need to spend months and perhaps years working in both Spanish and English, among books and records and among men and women, learning what has in fact occurred, and why it has occurred. What they learn should be recorded and shared with others. We do not need promotional reconstructions and dissertations on what ought to build up the Church according to such and such North American methodological, sociological, or theological assumptions. We need accurate accounts of how it has pleased God to multiply His churches in Mexico.

Finally, in whatever way it comes, there must be much more seeking of the lost where and when they can be found. All the knowledge in the world, truthfully recounted in many a monograph, is no substitute for seeking for the lost *until they be found*. Any church in Mexico will become a redemptive society as it yields itself to Him who walked the hills of Judea and Galilee seeking and saving the lost. That church, possessed by the Spirit of the Saviour, will walk the hills and valleys of Mexico, pound the sidewalks of its cities, and win the winnable while they are winnable. The function of knowledge is to illuminate the search, guide the findings, and turn those found and transformed into still other churches. These, maintaining close contact with their neighbors and kinfolk and proclaiming Christ, will in turn persuade still others to become the disciples of Him, whom to know is life abundant and eternal.

Index